JOHN LENNON

Recent Titles in Greenwood Biographies

JOHN LENNON

A Biography

Jacqueline Edmondson

GREENWOOD BIOGRAPHIES

 GREENWOOD

AN IMPRINT OF ABC-CLIO, LLC
Santa Barbara, California • Denver, Colorado • Oxford, England

Library of Congress Cataloging-in-Publication Data

Edmondson, Jacqueline, 1967–
    John Lennon : a biography / Jacqueline Edmondson.
        p. cm. — (Greenwood biographies)
    Includes bibliographical references and index.
    ISBN 978-0-313-37938-3 (print : alk. paper) — ISBN 978-0-313-37939-0 (ebook)   1. Lennon, John, 1940–1980.   2. Rock musicians—England—Biography.   I. Title.
    ML420.L38E36   2010
    782.42166092—dc22
    [B]   2010015232

ISBN: 978-0-313-37938-3
EISBN: 978-0-313-37939-0

14   13   12   11   10   1   2   3   4   5

This book is also available on the World Wide Web as an eBook.
Visit www.abc-clio.com for details.

Greenwood
An Imprint of ABC-CLIO, LLC

ABC-CLIO, LLC
130 Cremona Drive, P.O. Box 1911
Santa Barbara, California 93116-1911

This book is printed on acid-free paper ∞

Manufactured in the United States of America

To Luke, Jacob, and Michael, as always.

CONTENTS

CONTENTS

SERIES FOREWORD

In response to high school and public library needs, Greenwood developed this distinguished series of full-length biographies specifically for student use. Prepared by field experts and professionals, these engaging biographies are tailored for high school students who need challenging yet accessible biographies. Ideal for secondary school assignments, the length, format and subject areas are designed to meet educators' requirements and students' interests.

Greenwood offers an extensive selection of biographies spanning all curriculum-related subject areas including social studies, the sciences, literature and the arts, history and politics, as well as popular culture, covering public figures and famous personalities from all time periods and backgrounds, both historic and contemporary, who have made an impact on American and/or world culture. Greenwood biographies were chosen based on comprehensive feedback from librarians and educators. Consideration was given to both curriculum relevance and inherent interest. The result is an intriguing mix of the well known and the unexpected, the saints and sinners from long-ago history and contemporary pop culture. Readers will find a wide array of subject choices from fascinating crime figures like Al Capone to inspiring pioneers like Margaret Mead, from the greatest minds of our time like Stephen Hawking to the most amazing success stories of our day like J.K. Rowling.

While the emphasis is on fact, not glorification, the books are meant to be fun to read. Each volume provides in-depth information about the subject's life from birth through childhood, the teen years, and adulthood. A thorough account relates family background and education, traces personal and professional influences, and explores struggles, accomplishments, and contributions. A timeline highlights the most significant life events against a historical perspective. Bibliographies supplement the reference value of each volume.

OVERVIEW

John Lennon was a singer, songwriter, activist, artist, and writer whose life and work left an indelible mark on rock music and the world. Lennon first became famous as the founding member of the Beatles. His songwriting partnership with friend and bandmate Paul McCartney resulted in roughly 180 jointly written songs, and their collaboration remains among the most prolific and legendary in the history of rock music. The Beatles top *Rolling Stone*'s list of "Immortals: The Fifty Greatest Artists of All Time," which pays tribute to those bands and artists who had the most significant impact on rock and roll music. Lennon is the only solo Beatle ranked among the top 50. He is also ranked by *Billboard* as the second most successful songwriter in singles music history, following McCartney. Lennon's creative work, which extended beyond his years as a Beatle until the day of his murder on December 8, 1980, continues to inspire and provide enjoyment for millions around the world.

John Winston Lennon was born October 9, 1940, in Liverpool, England. He grew up in a quiet middle-class neighborhood, raised primarily by his aunt Mimi Stanley Smith. As a young boy, Lennon enjoyed American rock and blues music, including Elvis and Little Richard. He taught himself to play the guitar, often by listening to record albums over and over again until he mastered the chords. Lennon attended the Quarry Bank School and formed his first band, the Quarrymen, when he was 16 years of age. His band played at local community events in Liverpool. During a break between sets at one early performance, Lennon was introduced to Paul McCartney. Soon after, McCartney joined the band, and the two became fast friends. They spent as much time as possible together, playing songs and writing music. McCartney encouraged George Harrison to play guitar for Lennon, and once Lennon heard him, Harrison was invited into the band. Changes in the Quarrymen membership soon followed, and Lennon decided to change the band's name to the Beatles. The boys abandoned the skiffle music of the Quarrymen days and focused more on rock and roll. Just before they recorded their first single, Richard Starkey (aka Ringo Starr) joined the band.

The Beatles' first big break came in 1960 when they played backup for Johnny Gentle on a tour of the United Kingdom. This was followed by a six-week gig in Hamburg, Germany. Here the boys learned to play long sets and perfect their sound. When the Beatles returned to Liverpool, they became regulars at The Cavern, a basement club young people frequented. Record store owner Brian Epstein heard the Beatles perform at The Cavern and offered to become their manager. In 1963, the Beatles toured the United Kingdom and had their first number one hit, "Please Please Me." Soon Beatlemania swept the country, with throngs of screaming fans mobbing the boys at every venue. This only intensified when the Beatles embarked on their first tour of the United States in 1964, which included a performance on the Ed Sullivan television show that drew a recording-breaking 73 million viewers. The mop-top haircuts and clean-cut good humor enamored the boys to millions around the world, and they spent the next two years performing internationally, starring in movies, and, in Lennon's case, publishing two books. The queen appointed the Beatles as Members of the Order of the British Empire in 1965. By this time, Lennon had become disillusioned with fame and feared they had sold out to the establishment. He was weary of the constantly screaming fans who could not hear the Beatles music at live performances. The Beatles gave their last concert at Shea Stadium in 1966, and with the exception of an impromptu rooftop concert at their recording studio at 3 Savile Road in London, they performed only in the studio as they continued to record songs and release albums.

As the Beatles' popularity grew, they began to change their image and music, and they started to speak out on political and spiritual issues. The Beatles' hair grew long, they had beards and moustaches, and their clothes reflected their free-spirited nature. For a time, they engaged in transcendental meditation with the Maharishi Mahesh Yogi. Lennon experimented with sound in his music and began to create songs that helped to shape the psychedelic rock era, intentionally using feedback, distortion, and multitracking in his songs. Lennon spoke out against the Vietnam War, and he commented in an interview that the Beatles were more popular than Jesus. This soon turned public opinion, particularly in the United States, against him.

Lennon married fellow art student Cynthia Powell in 1963, and they had a son named Julian. Lennon continued to tour extensively with the Beatles and spent a great deal of time in the recording studio when he was not on the road. Lennon met Japanese avant-garde artist Yoko Ono at an art exhibit in 1966 and began a relationship with her soon after. Ono and Lennon became inseparable, adding to tensions among the Beatles, who were struggling with business decisions after Epstein's suicide in 1967. Ono joined Lennon when he was recording in the studio. The couple lived together in London until police raided their Montagu Square flat and confiscated a small amount of marijuana. Lennon pled guilty to drug charges to prevent Ono, who was pregnant with his child, from facing deportation. She miscarried soon after the arrest. Lennon divorced his first wife in 1968 and married Ono in 1969. The couple spent their honeymoon conducting bed-ins for world peace, first in Amsterdam and then in Montreal. They also began to create films and art exhibits together.

Lennon officially quit the Beatles in September 1969 as *Abbey Road*, was released. Lennon then turned his attention to his solo work, working in his recording studio at his home in Tittenhurst Park. In 1970 he released his first solo albums, *John Lennon/Plastic Ono Band*, which reflected his involvement with primal scream therapy, and *Imagine*. Shortly thereafter, Lennon and Ono left London to reside in New York City. The British press and Beatles fans had not been kind to Ono, and many blamed her for the Beatles' breakup. Once Lennon settled in New York, he continued writing and recording music. His first album after residing in the United States, *Some Time in New York City*, reflected his views on women's rights, race relations, and other political events. The couple became quite engaged in the political scene, participating in protests and speaking out against war and other injustices. This political activism created anxiety for the Nixon administration, and the U.S. government attempted to deport Lennon and Ono. Lennon fought the deportation case for several years until the U.S. court of appeals finally overturned the order in 1975.

Ono and Lennon separated in 1973, and Lennon moved to Los Angeles with May Pang, Ono and Lennon's personal assistant. This was one of the most creative times in Lennon's career as he focused on writing and recording. Three albums came from this period. Lennon frequented nightclubs and parties with friends, and at times his misbehavior became headline news. Lennon's final public performance was in November 1974, when he took the stage with friend Elton John to sing the duet "Whatever Gets You Through the Night."

In 1975, Lennon returned to New York and reconciled with Ono. The couple's son Sean was born in October, and Lennon largely retreated from public view for the next five years. Lennon spent time with son, learned to sail, and traveled with his family to Japan, Florida, and other places. In 1980, he returned to the recording studio and with Ono released the album *Starting Over*. There was much hope that Lennon was coming back into the music world with new creative energy, but this hope was cut short when Mark David Chapman shot and killed Lennon outside his New York apartment building on December 8, 1980. The world mourned his loss.

Lennon was a brilliant, impassioned, complicated, and creative man. His music lives forever through the Beatles, which remain among the most influential rock bands of all time, and through his creative solo work. Songs like "All You Need Is Love" and "Give Peace a Chance" remain anthems for peace, and his music is still played on radio stations around the world. Lennon was inducted into the Rock and Roll Hall of Fame in 1994; the Annex in New York City hosted a display of his writings, films, and personal memorabilia in 2009. In the years since his death, Ono has spoken out on Lennon's behalf against gun violence, and she continues to release Lennon's writing and music after his death through publications and various exhibits of his work.

INTRODUCTION

I remember when I heard the news that musician and former Beatle John Lennon was shot and killed outside his apartment building in New York City. I was 13 years old and recently had purchased his *Double Fantasy* album. I did not know much about Lennon at the time, but I liked some of his new songs that were playing on the radio. My parents listened to the Beatles when I was young, and I remember staring at the cover of *A Hard Day's Night* and wondering about these boys who made faces at the camera. The idea of John Lennon recording again interested me, as did the talk that Lennon was back, the habits and addictions that seemed to prevent him from recording music through much of the latter part of the 1970s behind him.

John Lennon was a unique and complex man, and he knew it. He once explained, "The only reason I am a star is because of my repression. Nothing else would have driven me through all that if I was 'normal.'"[1] Although he tried to distance himself from fans' adulation by saying he was just John Lennon, he knew he experienced the world differently than other people. He once explained, "I just see and hear *differently* from other people . . . and there is no way of explaining it."[2] What drove Lennon was an urge to create and, at least during some moments in his life, a desire to perform and to share his art with others—whether music, film, writing, drawing, or painting.[3] From the time he was a young boy, his imagination led him to places others could never dream, and this uninhibited creativeness resulted in music and other art forms that pushed boundaries and challenged the people who dared to engage it.

CONTEXTS

John Lennon grew up in the aftermath of World War II, which left both visible and invisible marks on his hometown of Liverpool. Eighty air raids on the city killed or injured thousands of people, and crumbled buildings and economic challenges left the city and its residents to deal with extensive devastation. Town rebuilding and port reconstruction began in the 1950s and continues to this day as Liverpudlians deal with ongoing economic challenges and urban planning demands. By the 1960s, Liverpool enjoyed renewed popularity as the center for the Merseybeat sound, largely due to the popularity of the Beatles and other Liverpool bands, and today the city still attracts a great deal of tourism as music fans flock to the city to see the sites and sounds associated with the world's most popular band.

In many ways, given the influence of American music on the Beatles, it made sense they hailed from Liverpool. From the time of the Civil War, ocean liners traveled between Liverpool and the United States on a regular basis, sharing music, stories, and culture. Liverpudlians sided with the South during the war, allowing it to open an embassy in the city.[4] While the docks were often a rough area populated with pubs and night clubs, and the industrial region had a reputation for radical politics and trade union militancy, the suburbs housed quiet middle-class communities. Travelers returning to Liverpool from New York and other American ports brought American artifacts with them, including record albums of American blues, country and western music, and folk music.

The 1950s were a time of change across Britain. National service was lifted, freeing youth from mandatory military duty, and young people who were born during or just after World War II were coming of age with new ideas about the world and their place in it. Like John

Lennon, many young people in Britain in the 1950s went to art school. It was a reasonable alternative for those who would not make it into college. In fact, many art students went on to be famous musicians: Pete Townshend, Keith Richards, Eric Burdon, and Ronnie Wood. Up to this point, there had been no real youth culture in England. Popular music primarily came from the United States, replete with musicians in suits or nice dresses crooning lovely tunes.

John Lennon was raised during a time when there were rigid understandings of gender and sexuality. Until 1967, it was illegal to be gay in Britain. Men, whether gay or straight, did not touch one another in public, and they did not openly display their emotions, at least not sadness or crying. It was widely accepted that a woman's place was in the home, where she cared for her husband and children. John was quoted as saying "women should be obscene and not heard"[5] in his prefeminist days, and whether or not he was joking, it is known that he was often violent and that women bore the brunt of his anger. It is well documented that he physically struck his first wife, Cynthia, when they were dating.[6] In the 1950s, some men felt it was acceptable to act this way. Brutality in the home was not grounds for divorce in England at the time, and so women who suffered this violence had few options.[7] This does not excuse John's behavior, and certainly not all men at this time acted in this way, but it does provide some social context for his actions.

At the time the Beatles began to record their music, young people had to go to record stores to buy albums. They most often listened to music on the radios or record players in their homes, on jukeboxes in restaurants and pubs, or at live concerts and performances. Music did not play continuously over stereo systems in shops or other public places like it does today, and certainly no one walked around in public enjoying private music experiences through iPods or other personal music devices.

When the Beatles began recording music, the 33⅓-rpm vinyl album and the 45-rpm vinyl single were about 20 years old. At the time, albums were described by the rotational speed at which they were played, called "rpm," or by their diameter, typically 12 inch, 10 inch, or 7 inch. The 33⅓-rpm vinyl album, which had a 12-inch diameter, was considered to be long playing and was often referred to as an LP.

The LP typically contained about 20 minutes of music on each side. The 7-inch 45-rpm (called a single) usually had one song on each side, with the song likely to be most popular and played on the radio on the A-side.

Record sales grew steadily from the late 1950s through the 1980s, primarily due to an increased youth market. The Beatles sold both singles and LPs, and the Beatles are attributed as a driving force in the popular music market; in fact, up until 1992, the only albums made before 1970 that sold more than seven million copies were Beatles albums.[8]

The Beatles revolutionized the recording industry in many ways, and John Lennon was in the lead as the group explored new and different sounds through their music. This was well before computers and advanced technologies made this work easier. When the Beatles began recording, there were single-track recorders, and later four-track and more advanced options. They experimented with ways to get more and different sounds by taking heads off the recorders, by using spinning speakers from inside the Hammond organ, and by experimenting with various sound effects and gadgets. The creative production of the Beatles albums is credited largely to producer George Martin. Working with sound technician Geoff Emerick, Martin transformed the studio from a simple recording room to a performance space where sound effects, overdubbing, and other technical tools were developed and honed.

UNDERSTANDING LENNON

John Lennon was complicated, brilliant, and riddled with contradictions. He pled with world leaders and the general public for peace while he privately struggled with a terrible temper and violence in his personal and family life. He lived with a lifetime of anger he attributed in part to his father's abandonment of him as a child, but he essentially did the same to his first son, Julian. John spent a great deal of his adult life struggling with his emotions as he tried to come to terms with pain and a sense of loss from his childhood. Beatles biographer Hunter Davies observed that "John's awfulness to people, his rudeness and cruelty, made people like him more."[9] Davies explained that John was the most original of the four Beatles.

From the time he was a young boy, John Lennon loved music. He was self-taught, first learning to play the harmonica and then the guitar. The musical influences on his early songwriting came from the Lonnie Donegan and the skiffle craze that took Liverpool by storm in the 1950s, as well as African American music and American blues. His contemporaries, including Paul McCartney, Mick Jagger, Bob Dylan, and later Elton John, pushed him in creative and interesting ways. As a boy, John went to his friends' homes to listen to the latest music from America, and then they played the songs over and over again on record players as they tried to master the chord progressions and lyrics. John's mother, Julia, encouraged him in these endeavors. She loved music and was a huge Elvis fan.

John formed his first band, the Quarrymen, with several of his friends when he was in high school. This group eventually included Paul McCartney and George Harrison, who later joined John with Ringo Starr as members of the Beatles. The Beatles went on to accomplish many firsts: they were the first band to write virtually all their own music, to create music videos, to intentionally use feedback on recordings, to use/be the subject of pop cartoons, to have three hit feature films, and to achieve simultaneous hits in dozens of countries. The band revived and enhanced the role of the electric guitar as they brought Motown, soul music, Jamaican reggae, and Indian sitar music to American and British audiences.[10] The songwriting duo of Lennon and McCartney remains one of the most productive and legendary in the history of music because of the number of songs they wrote and the continuing popularity of their music. Between 1962 and 1969, the pair wrote and published approximately 180 jointly credited songs. Twenty-six of these songs reached number one in the U.S. and/or U.K. charts, and 10 were listed in *Rolling Stone*'s 2004 list of top 100 songs. John was often dismissive of his public work with the Beatles, and he experienced conflicting feelings about whether they sold out by portraying themselves in ways that would sell albums and tickets at concerts. He later said of the band, "We were a band who made it big, that's all. Our best work was never recorded."[11]

Few could have imagined as the Beatles belted out songs in the nightclubs in Hamburg, Germany or The Cavern in Liverpool how famous these Liverpool boys would become, how much wealth they would amass (and generate for their hometown), or how long-lasting their fame would be. This fame was rife with complications, presenting challenges John could never imagine in his Quarrymen days. Fans screamed so loud at Beatles performances that they could not hear the music, prompting John to change the words to songs as a way to put some humor in the situation. Perhaps more disturbing, once the Beatles' music was public, they had little to no control over how it would be used or by whom. Some of the more troubling instances included murderer Charles Manson's references to the Beatles' music in the aftermath of the horrible slaying of actress Sharon Tate in 1969. Manson claimed he was inspired in this act by the Beatles' songs "Helter Skelter" and "Piggies." This was followed by bombings in New York in 1970 by a terrorist organization calling itself Revolutionary Force 9, causing police to question whether there was a Beatles connection, because of the Beatles' song "Revolution 9." John had no control of this, and the complications fame presented certainly troubled him.

In 2009, television and other news sources continued to cover the Beatles, sometimes almost daily. It was 40 years since the famous *Abbey Road* album was released, and fans spent the day imitating the famous album cover by crossing Abbey Road, some dressed as their favorite Beatle. Paul McCartney toured the United States. The Beatles' albums were reissued in a digitally remastered format. *The Beatles: Rock Band* videogame hit stores on September 9, 2009—the release date partly a recognition of John's favorite number, 9 (9/9/09). In the game, players could sing along with 45 tracks from the Beatles' career, and they could listen to previously unheard recordings of the band as they talked in the studio or view previously unseen photos of the boys. Ringo, Paul, Yoko, and Olivia Harrison, widow of the late George Harrison, all had a close hand in production of the game.

It is difficult to imagine whether John would have been amused or annoyed with this ongoing attention to a band formed half a century earlier. We do know that he was annoyed with the Beatles in the years after they disbanded, and he worked intentionally to change his physical appearance and public image to distance himself from that time. In the late 1960s and early 1970s, he used his celebrity in ways unlike other musicians at the time in order to address political concerns about peace, war, feminism, and human suffering. This came at great personal risk to him, professionally and personally. The public sometimes soured over his remarks and actions, and the FBI in the United States began a file to document his activities. He spent years battling efforts of the U.S. government to deport him from the United States, and he lived with government surveillance of his engagements as a peace activist. Lennon claimed he never missed the Beatles, but he spent time in the studio working on his last album reminding the musicians of his connections with the group. After his death, Paul explained that John was full of bravado and would never admit that he missed the Beatles. Paul was sure he missed them.

LEGACY

> Had there been no Beatles and no Epstein participation, John would have emerged from the mass of population as a man to reckon with.[12]

From the time John Lennon was a young boy, he imagined that he would die a violent death. As his fame grew, he anticipated that he would be "popped off by some looney."[13] But he never let this fear paralyze him or keep him from doing what he wanted. He once explained, "I'm not afraid of dying. I'm prepared for death, because I don't believe in it. I think it's just getting out of one car and getting into another."[14] But he never could have anticipated just how soon or suddenly his death would come, in the midst of a creative comeback on the music scene and planning for the future with his wife, Yoko Ono.

Fans who mourned John's death refused to accept that he was gone, and some carried signs that claimed "John Lives." In many ways he still does live on through his music and art. In the years after his death, Yoko carefully and systematically continued to release music, writing, and art that John created, and in 2009 she constructed an exhibit of personal items, creative pieces, music, and film in the Rock and Roll Hall of Fame Annex in New York City that caused fans to both laugh and cry. The exhibit allowed close-up views of intricate collages John created as gifts for Ringo and others, and it provided an opportunity to see the piano, complete with cigarette burns, that John used to write music when he lived at the Dakota, his apartment building in New York City. At the end of the exhibit, in an enclosed glass case, sat the brown paper bag filled with John's clothing and personal effects, just as it had been returned to Yoko from the hospital after his death. She never opened it, and as a piece in the exhibit it conveyed a message about the cold and impersonal brutality of murder. John Lennon was the 701st victim of armed assault in New York in 1980.[15] In the year preceding John's death, 10,700 people died from gunshot wounds in the United States. Next to the stark brown bag in the exhibit was a large white poster where people could sign their names as part of an effort to control guns and gun violence in the United States. This was not unlike Yoko's message on the 20th anniversary of John's death when she had billboards installed across the United States with the image of John's broken and bloodied eyeglasses on a windowsill and a statement that since his murder, 676,000 people had been killed as a result of gun violence in America. Others used John's murder to struggle against gun violence, including his friend Harry Nilsson. Nilsson organized events at Beatlefest conventions to raise money to fight gun violence.

Yoko's tributes to her husband extended beyond statements about gun violence. In 1980, John and Yoko established the Spirit Foundation to help people throughout the world. In the aftermath of John's death, Yoko asked grieving fans to contribute to the foundation in lieu of sending flowers. She primarily allocates the money to various humanitarian causes, including school-building projects in China and Africa, nonprofit organizations that support people who are living with AIDS, and efforts that support children and women.

In 1985, to commemorate what would have been John's 45th birthday, Yoko arranged to have 2.5 acres of land in Central Park named "Strawberry Fields" in John's memory (after the song "Strawberry Fields Forever," written by Lennon). The land is just across the street from the Dakota, and includes a large round mosaic with the word "Imagine" in the center. Fans often leave flowers, candles, and other memorabilia in the space to honor John.

John's former bandmates have also offered tributes to him over the years. In May 1981, George Harrison released the song "All Those Years Ago," a single about his time with the Beatles. He originally recorded the song a month before John was killed, but he rewrote the lyrics in honor of John after his death. The remaining members of the Beatles joined him in the recording: Ringo was on drums, and Paul sang backup with his wife Linda. The accompanying video consists of photos and short clips of John and the Beatles. A year later, Paul's *Tug of War* album (1982) included the song "Here Today," a tribute to John. On John's 50th birthday, Paul was on tour and he included a medley of John's songs in his lineup as a tribute to him, including "Strawberry Fields Forever," "Help!," and "Give Peace a Chance."

John's accolades and honors did not end when he died. In 1982, his *Double Fantasy* album won a Grammy for best album. The Beatles were inducted into the Rock and Roll Hall of Fame in 1988. In 1992, John received the Grammy's Lifetime Achievement Award, and in 1994, he was inducted into the Rock and Roll Hall of Fame as a solo artist.

Perhaps one of the most poignant tributes came from Julian Lennon, John's son with his first wife, Cynthia. In 2009, Julian established the White Feather Foundation to embrace environmental and humanitarian issues and help to raise funds for the betterment of all life. The foundation's name has a personal meaning to Julian, one that he explains in the pages of the Web site:

> Dad once said to me that should he pass away, if there was some way of letting me know he was going to be ok—that we were all going to be ok—the message would come to me in the form a white feather. Then something happened to me about ten years ago when I was on tour in Australia. I was presented with a white feather by an Aboriginal tribal elder, which definitely took my breath away. One thing for sure is that the white feather has always represented peace to me.[16]

Julian seems to be taking some lessons from his father as he attempts to use his celebrity and resources to try to make the world a better place.

Thirty years after John Lennon's death, his music still has a significant influence. At any given time, at least three radio stations around the world are playing a Lennon-McCartney tune.[17] The Beatles' albums still top the charts and are listed among the best albums of all time in *Rolling Stone*. In August 2006, the BBC's *Radio Club* celebrated its 50th anniversary. As part of the commemoration, it invited the British public to vote for its favorite album from across the years the club existed. More than 200,000 completed the survey. Four Beatles albums made the top 10, and *Sgt. Pepper's Lonely Hearts Club Band* topped the list.

John Lennon's murder on December 8, 1980, outside his home at the Dakota in New York City, brought a tragic end to one of the world's most creative individuals, but it did not end the tremendous influence his music, art, and life have had on the world. His work pushed boundaries and challenged norms, and his story inspires us to do the same.

NOTES

1. Elizabeth Thomson and David Gutman, *The Lennon Companion: Twenty-Five Years of Comment* (New York: Schirmer Books, 1987), p. 169.

2. Elizabeth Partridge, *John Lennon: All I Want Is the Truth* (New York: Viking Press, 2005), p. 15.

3. John Robertson, *The Art and Music of John Lennon* (New York: Carol Publishing Group, 1991), p. x.

4. Philip Norman, *John Lennon: The Life* (New York: Harper Collins, 2008), p. 23.

5. Robertson, p. 45.

6. Norman, p. 160.

7. Oliver Julien, *Sgt. Pepper and the Beatles: It Was Forty Years Ago Today* (Hampshire, England: Ashgate Publishing Company, 2008), p. 17.

8. Ibid., p. 157.

9. Hunter Davies, *The Beatles* (New York: McGraw Hill Publishing, 1985), p. liv.

10. Phil Strongman and Alan Parker, *John Lennon and the FBI Files* (London, England: Sanctuary Publishing, 2003), p. 12.

11. Geoffrey Giuliano and Brenda Giuliano, *The Lost Lennon Interviews* (Holbrook, MA: Adams Media Corporation, 1996), p. 34.

12. Brian Epstein, as quoted in Thomson and Gutman, p. 36.

13. Robert Fontenot, "Did John Lennon Have Any Signs of His Impending Death?", http://oldies.about.com/od/oldieshistory/f/lennon death.htm (accessed December 14, 2009).

14. Giuliano and Giuliano, p. 34.

15. Thomson and Gutman, p. 220.

16. Julian Lennon, How it all Started—The White Feather Foundation Meaning, 2009, http://www.whitefeatherfoundation.com/site/about/index.htm (accessed April 21, 2010).

17. Strongman and Parker, p. 170.

ACKNOWLEDGMENTS

Writing a book is never a solitary act, and I need to give special thanks to those who discussed this project with me and helped me to consider what should be included, particularly Jeremy Cohen, Murry Nelson, Patrick Shannon, and Peter Buckland.

I also want to express special thanks to Michael, Jacob, and Luke, who put up with me listening to the Beatles and John Lennon music for countless hours as I worked on this project. It was wonderful to have their company and enthusiasm as we walked the streets of New York City to see where John Lennon lived and worked, and it was particularly nice to have Luke join me at the Annex to experience the John Lennon exhibit. One of my favorite memories from this time is hearing Jake play *Abbey Road* on vinyl from his bedroom as I finished the book. I hope they will always have some interest in Lennon's music and an appreciation for his creative work.

TIMELINE: EVENTS IN THE LIFE OF JOHN LENNON

1906	Mimi Stanley, who would later raise John Lennon, is born in Liverpool, England.
December 14, 1912	Alfred Lennon, John Lennon's father, is born in Liverpool, England.
March 14, 1914	Julia Stanley, John Lennon's mother, is born in Liverpool, England.
June 28	Archduke Franz Ferdinand of Austria is assassinated, and events that follow lead to World War I.
1916	John "Bobby" Dykins, father to John Lennon's stepsisters, Julia and Jacqueline, is born.
November 11, 1918	The Armistice Treaty is signed, bringing an end to World War I.
1921	Jack Lennon, John Lennon's grandfather, dies. John's father Alf is sent to an orphanage with his sister Edith.
February 18, 1933	Yoko Ono is born in Tokyo, Japan.
1938	The Munich Agreement is signed.

December 3	Alf Lennon and Julia Stanley marry at the Liverpool Register Office. Three days later, Alf signs up for a three-month tour of duty on a cargo ship headed for the West Indies.
1939	Germany invades Czechoslovakia and Poland. France and Britain declare war on Germany.
September 10	Cynthia Powell is born.
July 7, 1940	Richard Starkey (aka Ringo Starr) is born in Liverpool.
October 9	John Winston Lennon is born in Liverpool.
May 1941	Blitz air raids on Liverpool cause extensive damage to the city.
June 18, 1942	Paul McCartney is born to Jim and Mary. Julia Lennon turns over care of her young son to her sister Mimi and her sister's husband, George.
1943	John's maternal grandmother, Annie Stanley, dies.
February 25	George Harrison is born to Louise and Harold Harrison.
February 4, 1944	British, U.S., and Soviet leaders meet in Yalta to determine postwar occupation of Germany.
April 12	U.S. President Franklin D. Roosevelt dies. Harry Truman becomes president.
April 28	Mussolini is killed.
April 29	German forces surrender.
April 30	Hitler commits suicide.
June 19, 1945	Julia gives birth to daughter Victoria. The baby is adopted by a Norwegian family.
August 15	Japan surrenders, ending World War II.
September	John begins school at Dovedale Primary. The U.S. drops atomic bombs on Hiroshima and Nagasaki.
1946	Julia begins long-term relationship with John "Bobby" Dykins.
1947	The Central Intelligence Agency is created in the United States, and the House Un-American Activities Committee begins hearings to rid the country of alleged communists.

March 5	Julia Lennon gives birth to daughter Julia.
October 26, 1949	Julia Lennon gives birth to daughter Jacqueline.
1950	John earns his beginner swimmer's certificate.
1952	John is a student at the Quarry Bank High School for Boys.
1953	Queen Elizabeth's coronation is held. J.D. Salinger publishes *Catcher in the Rye,* and the film *The Wild One* is released.
1955	The Teddy Boy craze surfaces in London. John adopts some of the fashion trends of this group, including the hair style and tight-fitting pants.
June 5	John's Uncle George, age 52, dies unexpectedly at home.
1956	Elvis releases "Heartbreak Hotel." John's mother buys him a guitar and John forms a band, the Quarrymen, with several of his friends.
July 1957	John meets Paul McCartney at the Woolton Parish Church during a Quarrymen performance. He invites Paul to join his band.
September	John begins his first term at Liverpool College of Art.
October 18	Paul plays with the Quarrymen for the first time.
November	Buddy Holly and the Crickets' song "That'll Be the Day" tops the UK singles chart.
March 1958	Elvis Presley is drafted into the U.S. Army.
July 15	Julia Lennon is killed after being struck by a car.
	John writes his first song "Hello Little Girl." George Harrison joins the Quarrymen.
1959	Buddy Holly is killed in a plane crash in February.
1960	John forms a music group with Paul McCartney, George Harrison, and Stu Sutcliffe. Pete Best joins later as drummer, and the band is initially called the Silver Beatles.

April 17	American singer Eddie Cochran dies in a car crash while on tour in the United Kingdom, just a few weeks after John, Paul, and Cynthia saw him perform in Liverpool.
August	The Beatles begin a six-week gig in Hamburg, Germany. In the fall, the Beatles make their first professional recording with Rory Storm and the Hurricanes, a Liverpool band.
March 21, 1961	The Beatles debut at The Cavern in Liverpool.
October	John and Paul travel to Paris to celebrate John's birthday.
November	Record store owner Brian Epstein stops by The Cavern to hear the Beatles perform.
1962	Brian Epstein becomes manager for the Beatles.
April	John's friend Stu Sutcliffe dies from a brain hemorrhage.
June	The Beatles sign with EMI records and they enter the studio on June 6 to record four songs.
August 23	John marries Cynthia Powell.
October	The Cuban Missile Crisis puts the world on the brink of nuclear disaster.
1963	The Beatles embark on their first UK tour.
March 2	*Please Please Me* hits number one on the British charts.
April 8	John Charles Julian Lennon is born to John and Cynthia.
August 8	Yoko Ono and husband Tony Cox welcome daughter, Kyoko.
November 22	The Beatles' second album, *With the Beatles* is released, the same day President John F. Kennedy is assassinated in Texas. The London *Times* and the London *Sunday Times* call Lennon and McCartney the most outstanding English composers of the year.
February 1964	The Beatles embark on their first U.S. tour, headlining twice on *The Ed Sullivan Show*.

"I Want to Hold Your Hand" is the top record in the United States.

March "Can't Buy Me Love" tops the U.S. and British charts. The Beatles begin to film *A Hard Day's Night*. John's first book, *In His Own Write*, is published.

August The Beatles return to the United States for a 32-day tour, meeting Bob Dylan. Harold Wilson, Labour Party, becomes prime minister of England.

1965 John's second book, *A Spaniard in the Works*, is published.

February John passes the exam to earn his driver's license. Ringo marries his girlfriend, Maureen Cox. Buckingham Palace awards the Beatles Members of the Most Excellent Order of the British Empire.

July 29 *Help!* premieres in London.

December John "Bobby" Dykins is killed in an automobile accident.

January 1966 George Harrison marries Patty Boyd.

March John states that the Beatles are more popular than Jesus Christ, setting off a backlash against the band's work across the United States.

August 29 The Beatles perform their final concert tour performance at Candlestick Park in San Francisco.

September John acts in the film *How I Won the War*.

November John meets artist Yoko Ono at the Indica Gallery in London.

June 1, 1967 *Sgt. Pepper's Lonely Hearts Club Band* is released.

August 27 Beatles manager Brian Epstein dies from a drug overdose.

1968 The Beatles found Apple Corps as an attempt to control their business ventures. Assassinations of Robert Kennedy and Martin Luther King Jr.

along with race riots in the United States and violence in Paris, Mexico City, and other parts of the world provoke John to consider ways to promote peace. George Harrison convinces the Beatles to visit the Maharishi Mahesh Yogi in India.

January The Prague Spring in Czechoslovakia signaled a period of political liberation.

July John and Yoko opened their art exhibit "You Are Here" by releasing 365 helium balloons. British Prime Minister Harold Wilson legalizes homosexuality for adults over 21 years of age.

August 22 Cynthia files for divorce from John.

September Hunter Davies's biography *The Beatles* is published. John and Yoko are arrested after marijuana is found in their apartment.

November Yoko suffers a miscarriage.

November 22 *The Beatles* (aka *The White Album*) is released.

January 30, 1969 The Beatles perform together for the last time in an unannounced appearance on the rooftop of the Apple building in London.

February 3 Allen Klein becomes the Beatles' manager.

March 20 John and Yoko marry in Gibraltar. John changes his middle name to Ono.

Charles Manson's followers murder American actress Sharon Tate, an act Manson claims was sparked by the Beatles' songs "Helter Skelter" and "Piggies."

September *Abbey Road* is released. John and Yoko campaign for world peace by engaging in bed-ins in Amsterdam and Montreal and posting billboards in major cities around the world that read "War Is Over! If You Want It." John returns his Member of the Most Excellent Order of the British Empire medal

October Yoko suffers another miscarriage.

March 13, 1970	A terrorist organization calling itself Revolutionary Force 9 takes credit for three bombings in New York, causing police to question whether there is a Beatles connection.
April	The Nixon administration invades Cambodia.
April 10	Paul McCartney publicly quits the Beatles, and a few months later he brings a lawsuit against them.
May	John travels with Yoko to Los Angeles for primal scream therapy. The FBI begins its file on Lennon. At the end of the year, John debuts his first solo album, *John Lennon/Plastic Ono Band*.
1971	John records *Imagine* at his home in Tittenhurst Park.
September 3	John departs for New York, never to return to England again.
January 30, 1972	Bloody Sunday occurs as British soldiers kill 13 people in a civil rights protest march in Ireland.
March	John and Yoko are served with deportation papers.
May	FBI director J. Edgar Hoover dies.
1973	John and Yoko move into the Dakota apartment building near Central Park in New York City. Yoko Ono is granted the right to stay in the United States.
September	John and personal assistant May Pang leave New York City to live in Los Angeles.
November	John's album *Mind Games* is released.
1974	Richard Nixon resigns as U.S. president rather than face impeachment over the Watergate scandal. John records the album *Walls and Bridges*.
November 28	John makes his final concert appearance, at Madison Square Garden with Elton John.

1975	John returns to New York and reunites with Yoko. The Beatles' final dissolution is official.
February	John's album *Rock and Roll* is released.
May 11	A concert is held to celebrate the last troops leaving Vietnam, but John and Yoko do not attend.
October 5	John is granted U.S. residency when the U.S. court of appeals overturns his deportation order.
October 9	John and Yoko's son Sean Taro Ono Lennon is born. John begins a five-year period where he is largely out of the public eye.
October 24	John's album *Shaved Fish*, a compilation of singles, is released.
January 5, 1976	Former Beatles road manager Mal Evans is shot and killed by Lost Angeles police.
January 26	John's recording contract with EMI expires.
April 1	Alfred Lennon dies of cancer.
August 16, 1977	Elvis dies.
1978	Cynthia Lennon promotes her memoir *A Twist of Lennon*, which shared details of her life with John.
1979	The BBC aired a "Beatles Christmas," showing six of their films. George Harrison's autobiography published.
July 14, 1980	John sails for Bermuda.
August 4	John and Yoko begin recording work at the Hit Factory.
November	John's album *Double Fantasy* is released.
December 8	John is killed by assassin Mark David Chapman when returning to his home in the Dakota.
1981	George Harrison releases the song "All Those Years Ago" as a tribute to John. The Cavern Mecca opens on Mathew Street in Liverpool as the first permanent tribute to the Beatles. Mayor Ed Koch sets aside a section of Central Park to be designated "Strawberry Fields" in

John's honor. Yoko pronounces John's birth-date to be "International World Peace Day."

1987   John is inducted into the Songwriter's Hall of Fame.

1988   The Beatles are inducted into the Rock and Roll Hall of Fame.

December 1991   Mimi dies.

1992   John receives Grammy's Lifetime Achievement Award.

1994   John is inducted into the Rock and Roll Hall of Fame as a solo artist.

November 29, 2001   George Harrison dies from cancer.

2002   A BBC poll ranks John Lennon 8th among the 100 greatest Britons.

2003   *Rolling Stone* ranks *Sgt. Pepper's Lonely Hearts Club Band* as the greatest album of all time.

2004   *Rolling Stone* ranks John Lennon number 38 on its list of "The Immortals: The Fifty Greatest Artists of All Time."

2005   *Rolling Stone* ranks John Lennon number 5 on its list of "100 Greatest Singers of All Time." Yoko releases a book with tributes to John Lennon.

2009   Lucy O'Donnell Vodden, Julian's childhood friend who inspired his painting and later the song "Lucy in the Sky with Diamonds," passes away. Julian Lennon founds The White Feather Foundation to support environmental and humanitarian concerns.

May 12   Yoko opens an exhibit of John's personal belongings and creative work from his life in New York City at the Rock and Roll Hall of Fame Annex.

Autumn   Yoko Ono and Bag One Arts present "Imagine Peace" in remembrance of what would have been John's 68th birthday.

Chapter 1

LIVERPOOL LAD

The threat of German warplanes bombing the city of Liverpool did not keep Mimi Smith at home on the night of October 9, 1940. Mimi's younger sister Julia was giving birth, and Mimi had to go to her. As she darted through the streets on foot nearly two miles to the Oxford Street Maternity Hospital, Mimi could only wonder how things would turn out for her beautiful and free-spirited sister once she was faced with the responsibilities of motherhood. Julia's husband, Alf, was at sea working as a steward on an ocean liner, and Julia's middle-class family did not hold him in very high regard. Alf came from a poor family in Liverpool and, like Julia, he was carefree and often irresponsible. Mimi was not convinced either could care properly for a child.

When Mimi arrived at the hospital, she was relieved to learn that her sister was fine and had given birth to a healthy seven-and-a-half-pound baby boy. Mimi could not take her eyes off the blonde-haired baby—he was so beautiful.[1] Julia named the newborn John, in honor of his paternal grandfather who worked the shipyards in Liverpool before dying of liver disease in 1921, and Winston, after the prime minister of England who was leading his country through the horrors of war. Julia noticeably ignored her own father, George Stanley, when she named the baby.

Mimi's relief that Julia and the baby were fine would be short lived. As the mother and child returned home to their small flat in Liverpool, Mimi began to worry once again. One problem was that Liverpool was an operations center for the Battle of the Atlantic, a term Prime Minister Churchill had coined, and it soon was a major target of the German Luftwaffe's efforts in England, second only to the city of London. The sea campaign, which lasted six years and was the longest continuous military campaign of World War II, pit allied navies and air forces against the German U-boats and warships. The Liverpool Blitz began in late 1940 and extended until January 1942, with the worst bombing during the early part of May 1941, when over 1,700 people lost their lives. The center of the city and the Wavertree area experienced extensive damage to homes and buildings. The Liverpool docks were also bombed, resulting in damage to ships, railway tracks, and other structures around the harbor. Air raid sirens warned citizens of possible attacks more than 500 times during the war, and the city was bombed approximately 79 times. After the air raids, the citizens had to exert tremendous caution because unexploded bombs and crumbling buildings presented further threats. Because of newspaper censorship, many of the bombings went unreported or vaguely reported. This censorship was intended to serve two purposes: preventing the enemy from having information about the effects of the bombings and keeping public morale as high as possible.

Mimi felt Julia and the baby would be safer if they moved away from the center of Liverpool to the suburban area of Woolton. Tens of thousands of women and children had been evacuated from the city because of German bombings. Many of Liverpool's poor were crowded in substandard housing, and good portions of these neighborhoods experienced extensive devastation. Once Julia was safe in Woolton, she would be closer to Mimi, who could help if she needed anything for the baby, who was turning out to be quite a handful. Julia moved into a cottage owned by Mimi's husband.[2]

Mimi's other source of worry was Julia's lifestyle. Julia was the most beautiful of the five Stanley sisters, and she was certainly the most fun-loving and flirtatious. As American GIs flooded Liverpool, nightlife in the city became quite exciting and filled with reckless abandon. Julia loved to go out in the evenings, dancing at clubs and enjoying jazz music the Americans brought with them.[3] Julia did not want Mimi to know how often she was going out, and she could not afford a babysitter, so she often waited until John fell asleep and then slipped out of the house, leaving him home alone. The child sometimes woke up frightened and crying, and he did not have his mother there to comfort him.[4]

Julia was never sure when Alf would return home, and one day when she went to collect her monthly allotment from the shipping company that employed him, she was told there was no money. Alf had been arrested and was detained abroad.[5] Julia did not know when or if he would ever return, but she also did not seem too concerned with his whereabouts. Julia was enjoying a new romance with a young soldier named Taffy Williams. She went out regularly with Taffy, his friend John Dykins (who was called Bobby), and his girlfriend Ann. Since Dykins was a wine steward at a local hotel, he could provide fresh fruit, chocolate, and scotch whiskey for his friends, rare treats during the war.[6]

When Alf finally returned to Liverpool after an 18-month absence, he learned of Julia's affair and that she was expecting Taffy's child. Alf confronted Taffy, but conceded that he was willing to let Julia remain with the man because of the unborn child. Julia, who had enjoyed so many fun times with Taffy, confessed that she did not want to continue her relationship with the soldier. She knew Taffy did not want to look after John, and Julia was not willing to give up her son, so she ended her relationship with the soldier. A few months later, Julia gave birth to a baby girl she named Victoria. Because of pressure from her family, particularly her father, Julia decided to give the child up for adoption. The Stanleys did not want to have an illegitimate child in the family. A Norwegian family adopted the baby, and Julia never saw the child again.

Even though Julia loved her son dearly, her activities created an uncertain and unstable environment for the child. If he was not at home alone, he was shuffled among family members. While John was certainly doted upon and loved, the instability was not easy on the child. During Julia's pregnancy with Victoria, four-year-old John was sent to live with his uncle Sydney Lennon, his wife, and their eight-year-old daughter, Joyce. John stayed with this family in Maghull, a suburb of

Liverpool, for eight months. Sydney and his wife hoped they would be able to adopt the boy;[7] however, when Alf returned from sea, he took John home with him.

Alf wished to save his marriage and his family, even though he was well aware of Julia's indiscretions, but he finally realized this was not to be. Soon after Victoria's birth and adoption, Bobby Dykins, Taffy's friend, began to date Julia, and the Lennon marriage finally dissolved for good. Alf was devastated, Julia's family was distressed yet again, and the continued upheaval had a lasting impact on John. Alf returned to sea, and Bobby moved in with Julia and John at 9 Newcastle Road, in Woolton.

John did not like his new living arrangements, and he began to act out to express his distress and disapproval. One way he did this was by bullying other children in his kindergarten class at the Mosspits Lane Infants School in Woolton. Five-year-old John made fun of other children, especially those he perceived to be weaker than he was. He often taunted the girls, causing them to scream and run away in fright.[8]

When John was especially upset, he ran away from home. He tried to guess which tram to ride to go to Aunt Mimi's house, searching for the one with black leather seats.[9] Sometimes he guessed correctly and ended up on Mimi's doorstep. His aunt looked after him until his mother could take him back to Newcastle Road. Sometimes he was not so lucky and took the wrong tram, which meant he needed to be clever and find his way back home.

One time after John showed up on her doorstep, Mimi called Alf rather than Julia. Alf was about to set out to sea, so Mimi put John on the telephone with his father. John told Alf he did not like his new father, and he wanted Alf to come home.[10] Alf changed his plans immediately and took the boy to Blackpool, a famous beach resort, where they stayed for six weeks enjoying the sun and the beach. When Julia finally discovered where they were, she traveled to Blackpool to confront Alf and John. When she arrived, Julia created a devastating and impossible situation, insisting that John choose to live either with his father or with her. At first, John chose his father, and when Julia asked the same question a second time, John did not change his mind. As Julia began to walk away from her son and her estranged husband, John realized the enormity of his decision and ran after her crying.

John returned to Liverpool with his mother, and Alf departed for New Zealand, where he would remain throughout John's childhood.

Julia took John and returned to her home with Bobby. She began referring to herself as Mrs. Dykins, even though she never officially divorced Alf or married Bobby. Mimi was quite disturbed by Julia's living arrangements, and she took it upon herself to hire a social worker to have John removed from his mother's home. At first the social worker was not concerned; however, when Mimi pointed out that there was only one bedroom in Julia's home, which meant the boy slept in the same bed as Julia and Bobby, the social worker had John removed. John went to live permanently at Mendips, with Mimi and her husband, George, as his guardians.

MENDIPS

Mendips, located at 251 Menlove Avenue, was a semi-detached house, which distinguished its residents from others who lived in terraced or row houses. Inside the spacious three-bedroom home covered with knobby gray pebbles was a large staircase and a stained-glass window with a Tudor rose motif. All the windows in the house had stained-glass borders that were decorated with flowers. Although Mimi and George did not have live-in housemaids, the original owners did, and the electric bells that once summoned the servants to each room remained a curiosity in the home. The sitting room, which was always quite tidy, contained a radio the family listened to in the evenings and bookcases with leather-bound copies of Winston Churchill's writing, something John's friend Paul McCartney would later admire. As John grew older, he read each one in turn.

John quickly became attached to his Uncle George. He was a kind man and the primary male influence on John's life as a young boy. George taught John to read, often using the newspaper as the text for their lessons, and he showed him how to draw and paint with watercolors. George seemed to be quite proud of the young boy, and he was affectionate toward John, hugging him and kissing him as parents often do with young children. As the boy grew older, George took him to the movie theater, and sometimes when John was in trouble with Mimi and sent to his room as punishment, George would sneak up the stairs to deliver John's favorite comic book and a chocolate bar.[11] George's life had not always been easy, and he seemed to have empathy for this child who experienced so much instability and difficulties in his early years.

Mimi raised John with a toughness that was born of her sense of responsibility to do the right thing and her penchant for running an efficient household. Mimi was always home when John returned from school, and she served meals regularly, insisted on a regular bedtime for John, and required routine bath times. She had high expectations, teaching John to speak in ways that reflected his middle-class upbringing. She frowned on the Scouse accent that was commonplace in the poorer parts of Liverpool. There was always a cool distance between John and Mimi, but they loved one another.

As John settled into Mendips and his new life with Mimi and George, the war came to an end. Nearly 4,000 citizens of Liverpool were known to be dead, and another 70,000 were homeless. It took years for Liverpool to recover from the devastation of World War II, with rubble and craters from bombed buildings still visible in the 1950s. John seemed to be relatively unaffected by the war; indeed in later years it was the turbulent family life of his childhood that haunted him most. These personal traumas, more than the possibility of German warplanes bombing his home, were most immediate to him and the scars from his early family situations were the ones that would remain.

SCHOOL DAYS

After John moved into Mendips, Mimi enrolled him at the Dovedale Primary School. John was quite bright and soon earned the compliments of the head teacher, who was impressed with his reading and writing abilities. John's favorite subject was art, and his masterpieces were displayed on the school's walls.[12] The head teacher told Mimi, "That boy's as sharp as a needle . . . He can do anything as long as he chooses to do it."[13]

John had a quick and wry sense of humor, and he joked and teased quite a lot. But sometimes he could still be mean spirited. John bullied other children and played a lot of pranks. In spite of this, he had some close and loyal childhood friends. Ivan "Ivy" Vaughn, whose house overlooked the back garden at Mendips, quickly became one of his best friends. The two boys played together quite a lot once John moved into Mendips, and they devised clever ways to secretly communicate. They created a special whistle to let one another know when they were going out to play,[14] and they passed notes to each other using a tin can strung from John's tree house to Ivy's yard.[15]

John and Ivy were friends with another boy named Nigel Walley, who also lived near them. Their quick friendship made another boy, Pete Shotton, angry because he felt that Ivy and Nigel had been his friends before John moved into the neighborhood. One day Pete began to taunt John and call him "Winnie" because of his middle name. John tackled Pete and pinned him to the ground, making him promise to never call him that again. Pete agreed, but as soon as he was away from John, he began to call him Winnie again. John was angry at first, but soon could not help but smile at the boldness Pete showed. The two became close friends after this.

John was clearly the leader among his childhood friends. He was reckless and daring, telling dirty jokes and stirring up mischief. John challenged the other boys and never really seemed to care much about what he said or did.[16] John spent a good bit of time reading comic books and adventure stories, and these fueled his imagination when he was out with his buddies. One of his favorite adventure series involved the fictional character William Brown written by Richmal Crompton. The *Just William* series told of the 11-year-old William's adventures with his gang of friends known as the Outlaws. Soon, John's real-life friendships with Ivy, Nigel, and Pete mimicked those he read in the William Brown stories as the boys engaged in small acts of defiance and daring. Sometimes the boys purposely walked on grass if there was a "keep off the grass" sign. At other times they hung from trees over busy roads to see who could dangle their leg in front of a double-decker bus before pulling it away.[17] Inspired by fictional William, John wrote his own adventure stories and comics, making himself the hero of the story.

John's avid reading and experiments with writing developed into an intense interest in language play. The British are often know for their unique humor, and it was a time-honored tradition dating back to famous Brits like Edward Lear to apply one's intelligence toward being unbelievably silly. John was no exception. He devoured the Lewis

Carroll books *Alice's Adventures in Wonderland* and *Through the Looking Glass*. One of his favorite poems was "Jabberwocky." John enjoyed the portmanteau words, words that were blended together in meaning and sound. In the *Alice* book, the character Humpty Dumpty explained portmanteau words to Alice by giving examples like "slithy" (lithe and slimy) and "mimsy" (miserable and flimsy). John soon created many words like this to use in his own writing.

After dinner, John spent his evenings listening to the radio with George and Mimi, and he either read or worked diligently on *The Daily Howl*,[18] his own humorous account of daily life captured in stories, drawings, and poems that he shared first and foremost at school the next day with his best friend Pete.[19] One poem was a spoof on the American frontiersman Davey Crocket called "The Story of Davy Crutch-Head." Another was a twist on a popular Petula Clark song called "Once There Was a Valley," which John rewrote as "Once There Was a Valet." John recorded the weather in a similarly humorous way: tomorrow will be Nuggy, followed by Tuggy, Wuggy, and Thuggy.[20] He liked to use India ink with calligraphy pens as he wrote spoofs and created caricatures of his teachers and other adults.

When he was 11 years old, John passed the important Eleven Plus British school system examination, which earned him a bicycle from Uncle George. John was then admitted to high school at the Quarry Bank School, where he began studies in January 1952. The all-boy school was known for its academic excellence, especially in the humanities, and some referred to it as the Eton of the Labour Party. It proudly boasted of a few socialist prime ministers who were alumni of the school.

John's best friend Pete Shotton was also admitted to Quarry Bank, and both boys were placed in the "A" stream, the class reserved for students who were believed to be the most intelligent. Although John and Pete wore the same school uniform as the other boys—black blazers and caps, gray sweaters and pants, white shirts, and black ties with maroon and gold stripes—they were soon quite distinguishable from their peers. John adjusted his tie to be skinnier than the other students' ties, and his and Pete's ongoing pranks and lack of seriousness drew a great deal of attention to them. John was certainly bright enough to do well in school, but he chose not to. He had poor eyesight, but he refused to wear his eyeglasses, which only exacerbated his poor performance.

Rather than taking school seriously, John preferred to fool around with Pete. They rigged the blackboards so they collapsed when the teacher wrote on them, or they filled their bicycle pumps with ink to squirt on the other students on the playground.[21]

Over the years, the Quarry Bank punishment book documented the various insubordinations that Lennon and Shotton engaged in: gambling on the school field during a cricket match, throwing a blackboard eraser out the window, failing to report to the office, and, most often, cutting class and disappearing from school to smoke cigarettes, something the two friends discovered by their third year.[22] Sometimes the school head called Aunt Mimi to report on John's indiscretions, but they both knew there was little she could do. John was demoted to the "B" stream, and finally to the lowest track, the "C" stream,[23] but it did not matter to him.

TEENAGE YEARS

As John got older, he spent more of his free time away from Mimi. Sometimes he took the bus to downtown Liverpool to hang out at the Kardomah coffeehouse, where he sat sketching and watching passersby for hours on end. At other times, he went to his mother's house. Julia was witty and had a dry sense of humor, and John enjoyed her company a great deal. Bobby and Julia had two daughters together, Julia and Jacqueline, and they were always quite happy to see their older brother. Julia had one of the first televisions in the neighborhood, and John liked to watch it when he visited with her. They also enjoyed listening to music together. Julia cherished the time John spent with her, and she was often sad when he left to return to Mimi's.[24]

John was also quite close to his mother's three other sisters: Anne, Harriet, and Elizabeth. All were considered to be quite unconventional by the standards of their day. In post-World War I Britain, it was expected that women would marry at a young age and have children right away, and it was unthinkable that they should have aspirations that extended much beyond caring for a home and family, but none of the five Stanley sisters seemed too concerned with these norms.

Mimi, whose birth name was Mary, married George Smith relatively late in life when she was 33 years old. Before her marriage, she had a professional career as a nurse and a personal assistant. Mimi never gave birth to a child. Elizabeth, called Mater, married marine surveyor Charles Parkes, and together they had a son, Stanley. Mater was not sure she could care for Stanley, although she loved him dearly, and so she sent him to her own mother to be raised, and then later to boarding school. After Charles died, Mater married Robert Sutherland, a dental surgeon, but they did not have children together. Anne, who the family called Nanny, had a career as a civil servant, and she waited until she was 30 years of age before she married Sydney Cadwallader, a ministry official.[25] Together they had a son named Michael. Harriet, or Harrie, was the youngest of the sisters. She married an Egyptian named Ali Hafez, and after they wed, the couple moved to Cairo and had a daughter named Leila. After Ali died, Harrie returned to England with her young child and married Norman Birch of the Royal Army Service Corps. They settled in Edinburgh where the extended family typically gathered for holidays. Harrie and Norman had a son named David. Of all the Stanley sisters, Julia was of course the most beautiful and unconventional. There was always laughter and a lighter spirit when she was in the room.

The back door to Mimi Smith's kitchen at 251 Menlove Avenue swung open and closed with regularity as she and her four sisters gathered for lively discussions over a pot of strong tea with milk. Mimi became self-appointed matriarch of the family after the death of her mother, Annie, looking out for the well-being of her younger sisters and their children as best she could. As the women visited together, John and his cousins played in the garden or upstairs in John's bedroom. Stanley, Leila, and John were the oldest of what would eventually be seven cousins, and the younger children looked up to the older ones, especially John. His bedroom was fascinating to them. It was the only untidy place in Mimi's immaculately clean home. Books were strewn everywhere, including some that he was writing himself. As a boy, John hung a collection of paper skeletons and monsters over his bed that connected to a string that, when pulled, caused the scary creatures to dance and jiggle, much to the delight of the young children. As he got older, the skeletons were replaced with posters of his favorite movie stars, including Brigette Bardot.

John spent every summer with Mater and his cousins. As a young boy, he went to her townhouse at 15 Ormidall Terrace in Auld Rukie, and then as he grew older, he visited her at her sheep farm at San-gobeg near Durness on the northernmost coast of Scotland. John took the bus from Liverpool to Scotland, and on one of these jour-neys, he played his new harmonica the entire time. The bus driver was impressed with the boy's playing and gave him a nicer harmonica, a Hohner model someone left behind on the bus. John loved Scot-land and spent his time hiking and romping around the farm with his cousins.

Usually John was greeted warmly by Mimi and George when he re-turned from Scotland, but the summer before John's 16th birthday, he returned home to Mendips to face an unexpected tragedy. His beloved Uncle George had died of a massive hemorrhage caused by sclerosis of the liver while he was away. Mater had known what had happened but had not told John this sad news, and so he returned home without knowing about George's death. When John walked through the door at Mendips, happy to be home, he found Mimi crying in the kitchen. His reaction to the devastating news she told him was to laugh. He did not know what else to do.

Mimi sought consolation among her sisters, particularly Julia, after George died. Rather than face the emptiness and sorrow at Mendips, John spent more time with Julia at her home on Blomfield Road. His friends often joined him. They enjoyed Julia's free spirit, and they loved her sense of humor. Julia would sometimes do outrageously funny things. One time she walked down the street with a pair of eyeglasses that had no lenses. People did not immediately notice that the glasses had no lenses, and as they talked to her, she rubbed her eye by putting her finger through the empty frame.[26] John and his friends welcomed how Julia encouraged their rebellious attitudes, something Mimi and their parents would never consider.

YOUTH IN BRITAIN

In 1955, the Teddy Boy craze spread through London. The Teddy Boys were a group of young men who did not want to adopt the drab clothing and norms of their parents' generation. Instead, they wore tight-fitting pants called drainpipes that were tailored close at the ankle, chukka boots, and bright fluorescent orange or lime green socks. John began to dress like a Teddy Boy, styling his hair in a pompadour with long side burns and wearing an Edwardian lounge suit with a long jacket and velvet collar, although it is not clear that he was actually considered to be a member of this social group. "The Teds," as they were called, most often were working-class boys known to be juvenile delinquents.

In 1956, the American movie *Rock Around the Clock* was released. It featured Bill Haley and the Comets, and thrilled exuberant theatergoers in the United States and Britain. The Teds were fanatic about the film, and some Teds ripped up movie theaters all over London in their excitement. John was not particularly interested in *Rock Around the Clock*, although he went to see it.[27] Instead, he found inspiration in Elvis's music, including "Heartbreak Hotel." John first heard about Elvis from a classmate at Quarry Bank named Don Beatty,[28] and when Elvis followed "Heartbreak Hotel" with hit songs like "Blue Suede Shoes," and "Hound Dog," John was increasingly drawn into the American blues-influenced rock and roll music. He read everything he possibly could about this exotic new celebrity, and he sought out more songs from American blues artists. One consequence of this interest was that he talked endlessly about Elvis, driving Aunt Mimi a bit crazy with his running commentary. She later recalled, "It was nothing but Elvis Presley, Elvis Presley, Elvis Presley . . . In the end I said 'Elvis Presley's all very well, John, but I don't want him for breakfast, dinner and tea.'"[29] John had a poster of Elvis in his bedroom at Mendips, and he often stood in front of his mirror pretending to be Elvis.[30]

As he became more enthralled with American rock music, John desperately wanted to have a guitar, but Mimi would not allow it. She despised pop culture. John's mother, Julia, however, loved rock and roll, and she shared John's enthusiasm for Elvis. Julia even named a kitten purchased for John's half sisters after the American idol.[31] Julia spent 10 pounds to buy John his first guitar, a Gallotone Champion purchased through mail order from Headquarters and General Supplies in London.[32] The Gallotone was an acoustic guitar, an Old Spanish-style instrument with steel strings and a label inside that read "Guaranteed not to split." Because Julia could play banjo, she tuned John's guitar as she would a banjo, and then taught him a few chords. The first song John learned to play was Fats Waller's "Ain't It a Shame." John began to play guitar all the time, and he listened to rock music every chance he got, even hiding a small transistor radio under his bed covers at night so that he could listen to the music without Aunt Mimi knowing about it.[33] Mimi tired of John's incessant guitar playing, and she would not let him play in the house. Instead, he had to play in the glass-enclosed porch. Mimi explained to him, "The guitar's all very well, John, but you'll never make a living at it."[34] She worried that he was not preparing for his upcoming General Certificate of Education (GCE) exams.

Much as John admired Elvis, even styling his hair after the American rock star's pompadour (something Mimi disapproved of), John did not necessarily wish to become Elvis. Instead, he preferred Lonnie Donegan and the skiffle craze that was taking the Liverpool area by storm. Donegan was influenced by Huddie Ledbetter, also known as Lead Belly, one of the foremost figures of American blues music, known for his intense vocal performances and his skill on the 12-string guitar. Donegan's first hit was "Rock Island Line," a song associated with the blues legend.[35] Like Elvis, Donegan made black, blues-style music appealing to white youth, creating skiffle as a genre of street corner black jazz. Skiffle was also a more socially acceptable form of music than rock and roll, rising to the height of its popularity in the mid-to-late 1950s.[36] It was surprisingly easy to play, typically involving only three chords and an assortment of instruments that were commonplace.

Soon John begged Mimi to buy him a better guitar. She finally agreed, and the two went to Hessy's Shop in Liverpool, where Mimi paid £17 for the new guitar. Mimi was not excited about this, primarily because she preferred classical music and did not appreciate popular music, but she thought the guitar would keep John quiet and out of trouble.

John went to his friend Mike Hill's house every day at lunch so they could listen to American music. In addition to Elvis's new tunes, they listened to songs by Chuck Berry, Fats Domino, and Little Richard that made their way over the airwaves and through record stores to the United Kingdom. Little Richard's music had a tremendous impact on John, rendering him uncharacteristically speechless when he first heard it.[37] He enjoyed the nonsense and playful words in Little Richard's music, and Little Richard's screaming thrilled him. John also enjoyed music by Louisiana artist Larry Williams, including "Bad Boy," "Dizzy Miss Lizzy," "Bony Moronie," and "Slow Down"—songs he would later cover as a Beatle or in his solo work.

In March 1957, John Lennon formed his first band, a skiffle group called the Quarrymen, named after his school. John was lead singer and guitar player, and his friend Pete Shotton played washboard. Eric Griffiths, who acquired his first guitar around the same time as John, played guitar, and Rod Davies played banjo. Bill Smith played bass for a while, but was soon replaced by Len Garry, who also had an acceptable singing voice. Colin Hanton, Rod and Eric's friend, played drums. Although Colin was two years older than the other boys and not a Quarry Bank student, John was still the band's unquestioned leader. John decided what the boys would play and where. Colin had a drum set, an unusual luxury for a skiffle band, and he had the words "Quarry Men" stenciled on the side of his bass drum, splitting the band's name into two words so that it fit on the front of the drum.[38]

The band's music primarily consisted of three chords: C, G7, and F.[39] They played Donnegan songs, as well as popular tunes by the Vipers and Burl Ives. The boys learned the music by listening to 78-rpm records over and over again. When they were unable to determine the lyrics, John made them up. He believed that sound was the most important thing. The boys sometimes had trouble finding space where they could rehearse, but they could always count on a warm welcome from Julia. When they went to her house, she always listened as they shared stories of their latest adventures. Julia made tea for them, and allowed them to use her bathroom as a practice space because this room had the best acoustics in her house.[40]

The Quarrymen played their first professional performance near the Penny Lane roundabout at the St. Barnabas Church Hall during the fall of 1956. Not much is known about this event, including the exact date, but Julia went to hear the boys perform, as did John's girlfriend Barbara Baker.[41] John had to sing loudly to be heard over his bandmates since there was no microphone, and he refused to wear his glasses, which made it difficult for him to see the edge of the stage. To the audience, John appeared to be aggressive and challenging, with his slightly hunched stance and squinted eyes.

The Quarrymen performed again on June 22, 1957, as part of a citywide celebration commemorating King John granting Liverpool its charter in the 13th century, playing two sets from the back of a flatbed truck. John's mother and half sisters Julia and Jackie were in the audi-

John Lennon performs on stage with his first band, the
Quarrymen, at a church function in Woolton, Merseyside,
Great Britain, July 6, 1957. (AP Photo/Str.)

ence. Photos from this event are the first of John performing onstage,
wearing a pompadour hairstyle and a plaid cowboy shirt Julia bought
for him.

Soon after, on July 6, 1957, the Quarrymen played at St. Peters'
Church garden fete in Woolton. They played outdoors, performing
Lonnie Donegan's songs "Cumberland Gap" and "Railroad Bill," along
with their own version of the Liverpool folk song "Maggie May." After
the outdoor performance, they set up in the social hall for the evening
show where the boys entertained the crowd with other songs that were
popular among the young people in attendance at the event.

John's childhood friend Ivy Vaughan attended the event with his
good friend, a 15-year-old boy named Paul McCartney. During a break
in the show, Paul kindly offered to tune John's guitar, something John
was uncertain how to do, and then he casually began to play Eddie

Cochran's hit "Twenty Flight Rock" and Gene Vincent's "Be-Bop-a-Lula." John was impressed but had some reservations about taking Paul into the group:

> I half thought to myself, "He's as good as me." I'd been kingpin up to then. Now, I thought, "If I take him on, what will happen?" It went through my head that I'd have to keep him in line if I let him join.[42]

Later, John remembered that he asked Paul to join the band at this event, but others report that it was really Pete Shotton who, at John's request, invited Paul into the group a few weeks later.

Paul became John's guitar tutor, something that was not particularly easy because Paul was left handed. Paul could tune a guitar, and he knew the lyrics to dozens of hit songs.[43] The two studied Bert Wheedon's guitar instruction manual, but they were not able to really watch and study someone else playing a guitar. Aunt Mimi did not approve of John's friendship with Paul because Paul was from the working class, but this did not deter John. Mimi never approved of any of his friends, except perhaps Nigel, whose father was a police sergeant.[44] But Paul's father did not approve of Paul's friendship with John either. He thought John would get Paul into trouble. Julia was another story. She liked Paul and felt sorry for him that he had lost his mother at such a young age.

There were similarities between the two boys. They both had Irish ancestry, and both of their fathers had an interest in music. Jim McCartney led a small dance band, and he played the piano, and Alf loved to sing and perform. Both boys were artistic and intellectual, and both loved to read. Paul enjoyed the Richmal Crompton *Just William* books, and he could quote Chaucer and Shakespeare. They shared an enjoyment for nonsense, from Lewis Carroll to the *Goon Show*, a popular radio comedy show that ran from 1951 to 1960, full of absurd plots, puns, and silly sound effects.

But there were clearly differences between Paul and John as well. John was raised in the middle class, while Paul was considered to be working class, no small matter in England where class distinctions remained strong. Perhaps even more apparent were differences in their personalities. John flew off the handle or sulked when he was angry, while Paul engaged in "sneak attacks."[45] Paul was not reckless like John.

When Paul joined the Quarrymen, he attempted to make some changes in the band. Some happened: the boys began to dress in a similar, more professional style, with matching black jeans, white shirts, and Western boot-lace ties.[46] Other suggestions were not realized: changing the share manager Nigel Wally received to a lower rate, or getting rid of Colin Hanton, whose drum playing was inadequate for Paul.

The Quarrymen began to play a regular gig at Charles McBain's at the New Clubmoore Hall in Norris Green, a residential area in Liverpool, and the Wilson Hall in Garston, a constituency in the southern part of Liverpool. Garston had a reputation for drawing a tough crowd of local Teds, and they loved rock and roll music. John was happy to oblige, particularly now that Paul was part of the band and could sing the Eddie Cochran, Jerry Lee Lewis, and Little Richard numbers the audience wanted to hear.[47] One consequence of the shift to rock music was that the Quarrymen no longer needed Pete Shotton to play the washboard, and he soon left the band, spending less and less time with John as Paul and John's relationship developed. Paul and John began to distance themselves from the other Quarrymen as well, holding practice sessions on their own, often at Paul's house on Forthlin Road, just a minute's walk from Julia's place. Here the two would spend time playing guitars, writing music together, and listening to the radio, including Buddy Holly and the Cricket's new single that was topping the UK charts in November 1957—"That'll Be the Day." Holly's influence on the boys was both musical and stylistic. They learned the simple chord progressions and vocal backups Holly used, and they incorporated similar structures into their early music. John asked Mimi to buy him a pair of eyeglasses similar to the large black horn-rimmed glasses Holly wore, although once he had them, he only wore them when absolutely necessary.

In the spring of 1957, John failed all seven of his GCE O-level exams (ordinary exams), including English and art—subjects in which his teachers believed he showed the most talent.[48] Passing scores were required to earn the general certificate in education and matriculate to a college or university. John had not given much thought to what he would do next, although he thought he could become famous as an artist and he was sure he wanted to be a millionaire.[49] He made a vain attempt to enroll in a training course with his friend Nigel that would allow him become a ship steward, but he needed consent from his guardian, something Mimi would not grant. His relationship with Barbara was over, and she began a relationship with one of John's friends and became pregnant. John was quite upset when he heard the news, and he offered to marry her.[50] She refused and went to Liverpool to have the child. After she gave the baby up for adoption, John and Barbara briefly resumed their relationship, but things had changed between them, and the relationship did not last long.

Mimi tried to determine what would be next for John. She likely discussed this with her sisters over tea at the kitchen table, and she decided to consult with the Quarry Bank School's headmaster, Mr. Pobjoy. Art had been John's best class at Quarry Bank School, and he seemed to have some potential for it. John enjoyed drawing using India ink on white paper. His drawings were influenced by popular British comic artists like Ronald Searle, whose work appeared in popular magazines and newspapers, and American James Thurber, who drew for the *New Yorker*. Mr. Pobjoy suggested art school and wrote a letter to help John get accepted to the Liverpool College of Art. Mimi depleted her savings to send him to the school (£2,000).

NOTES

1. Albert Goldman, *The Lives of John Lennon* (New York: William Morrow and Company, 1988), p. 26.

2. Ibid., p. 28.

3. Philip Norman, *John Lennon: The Life* (New York: Harper Collins Publishers, 2008).

4. Goldman, p. 30.

5. Ibid.

6. Ibid., p. 31.

7. Norman, p. 18.

8. Goldman.

9. Ibid., p. 34.

10. Ibid.

11. Elizabeth Partridge, *John Lennon: All I Want Is the Truth* (New York: Viking Press, 2005).

12. Ibid.

13. Norman, p. 34.

14. Geoffrey Giuliano and Brenda Giuliano, *The Lost Lennon Interviews* (Holbrook, MA: Adams Media Corporation, 1996), p. 191.

15. Norman, p. 43.

16. Partridge, p. 21.

17. Norman, p. 51.

18. In 1988, three pages of *The Daily Howl* were auctioned by Sotheby's in London for £12,000.

19. Bill Harry, "The Daily Howl," *Mersey Beat*, March 12, 1964. http://www.triumphpc.com/mersey-beat/archives/dailyhowl.shtml (accessed December 26, 2009).

20. Ibid.

21. Partridge, p. 18.

22. Norman, p. 62.

23. Norman, p. 61.

24. Norman, pp. 56, 57.

25. Julia Baird and Geoffrey Giuliano, *John Lennon, My Brother* (New York: Henry Holt and Company, 1988), p. 5.

26. Hunter Davies, *The Beatles* (New York: McGraw Hill Publishing, 1985), p. 17.

27. Norman, p. 76.

28. Ibid., p. 79.

29. Ibid., p. 82.

30. Goldman, p. 63.

31. Norman, p. 83.

32. Ibid., p. 88.

33. Ibid., p. 85.

34. Ibid.

35. Ibid., p. 86.

36. Ibid.

37. Partridge, p. 29.

38. Norman, p. 91.

39. Goldman, p. 65.

40. Norman, p. 95.

41. Ibid., p. 93.

42. Goldman, p. 68.

43. Cynthia Lennon, *John* (New York: Crown Publishers, 2005), p. 31.

44. Partridge, p. 21.

45. Goldman, p. 69.

46. Norman, p. 117.

47. Ibid.

48. Mike Evans, as quoted in Elizabeth Thomson and David Gutman, *The Lennon Companion: Twenty-Five Years of Comment* (New York: Schirmer Books, 1987), p. 15.

49. Norman, p. 110.

50. Ibid., p. 111.

Chapter 2

THE ARTIST

Mimi hoped John's interests and habits would become more refined once he attended art school.[1] If John completed the Liverpool College of Art program, he would earn a National Diploma in Art and Design. Mimi expected this could lead to some form of respectable middle-class employment for the boy. The curriculum was much like that of other art colleges at the time: the first two years of study engaged a broad range of subjects, including architecture, lettering, and art history, followed by an exam to determine a specialist field, such as painting or sculpture, for the final two years of study.

To his disappointment, John found the schedule at the art school to be very similar to the routines at Quarry Bank School. Attendance was called promptly each morning, followed by long hours in the classroom. John did not like the schedule or the confinement, and he quickly resumed his old habits of pulling pranks and getting into trouble. Soon his instructors were expecting very little from him, and some were even intimidated by his behavior and antics, including the sculpture tutor Philip Hartas, who described John as "a fellow who seemed to have been born without brakes."[2] One exception was art teacher Arthur Ballard, who made an effort to spend extra time with John. The two sometimes went to a club called the Basement in Mount Pleasant to talk. Ballard nearly gave up hope that he could reach John until he accidentally found John's sketchbook, carelessly left behind in an empty lecture room. The book was filled with caricatures and drawings, poems, and satirical comments, giving Ballard insight into John's creative and witty nature.[3] Ballard discussed the work with John, who seemed surprised by his teachers' enthusiasm and interest.

Since Paul McCartney's school was next door to the art college, John tried to get together with him as often as possible. They practiced during lunch and other short breaks in the schedule, even though it was against school rules. The two continued to write songs every chance they could, sometimes cutting out of school early to work on their music at the McCartney house at 20 Forthlin Road. Paul grasped the structures of music rather quickly, and John was particularly masterful at lyrics, and their songwriting partnership would develop into one of the most prolific and successful in the world. Both contributed extensively to the music and the lyrics of the songs they wrote during this time, rather than clearly delineating a role for each partner, and they spent countless hours bouncing ideas back and forth, trying to one-up the other in a healthy competitive spirit. John and Paul wrote about 100 songs during their first year together, establishing collaborative patterns that continued for the next decade. As they jotted down their ideas, they were careful to attribute the new song as "Another original by John Lennon and Paul McCartney."[4]

Since the boys had no tape recording devices, they could only keep track of their music by noting ideas in an exercise book. They decided that if neither one of them could remember the music the next day, the song was no good and they should scrap it.[5] Some of these early songs are long lost, but others were later recorded: "Love Me Do," "Hello Little Girl," and "One after 909." John later explained that "Hello Little Girl" was his first song, and that its influences were traced back to "Delightful, Delicious, De-Lovely." Buddy Holly's influence on John's music is evident in the piece, including a middle section of the original song that was borrowed from Holly's 1958 hit "Maybe Baby."[6]

Paul wished to have his schoolmate, George Harrison, join the Quarrymen, and he suggested this idea to John. George had been following the Quarrymen for about a year and so he knew their music well. John did not know much about George or his playing, so one night when the three boys were on the top deck of an empty late-night bus, Paul encouraged George to play the hit song "Raunchy" for John. George played it perfectly, and John was surprisingly impressed. He decided to take the boy into the band. Later when Aunt Mimi found out, she expressed her disapproval of John's bandmates, and she made a point of complaining about George's style of dress, his broad Scouse accent, and his lower social status (George's father was a bus driver).[7] As usual, John shrugged off Mimi's concerns; George could play guitar and that was all that mattered to John.

Soon George was practicing solos on his cello-style Hofner President guitar. George was serious and earnest, in stark contrast to John's prankster personality, and this combined with the two-and-a-half years between them kept the two at a bit of a distance at first. George was clearly in awe of John, but he could talk back to John's insults, so John soon warmed to him.[8] George was tenacious, mastering chords and working for hours on end until he was able to play something perfectly.[9] It did not take long for John to realize that musically George was a "kindred spirit."[10]

To make room for George in the band, which now had four guitar players, John decided to drop the less-accomplished Eric Griffiths, the last of the original Quarrymen band members. Bass player and singer Len Garry had departed earlier because of health problems. Although the changes in personnel were intended to improve the Quarrymen, the group was offered fewer and fewer gigs throughout 1958, and at times they nearly became extinct.[11]

The boys had no clear sense of how they sounded to others since they were unable to record themselves playing. One solution was to pay a professional studio to record them on a gramophone record. The recording could also help them to advertise for new gigs. They decided to give this a try, and in mid-1958, John, Paul, George, Colin Hanton, and one of Paul's piano-playing friends named Duff Lowe pulled together enough money for Percy Phillips, who ran a recording studio in his house in Liverpool, to record them. The boys had just one take, and their efforts resulted in one 45-rpm size record with a song on each side:[12] Buddy Holly's "That'll Be the Day," with John singing lead vocals, and "In Spite of All the Danger," a country-western style song

Paul wrote with a co-credit to George for the guitar solo. Even though their friend Nigel Wally played the album around town, it did not help to increase business for the band. John was disappointed, but soon his attention would be taken up with a deeper sorrow.

LOSING JULIA

July 15, 1958 promised to be like any other day during John's summer break from art school. He woke at Mimi's house, and later in the day he went off with some friends before heading to Julia's home. John enjoyed a good relationship with his mother that seemed only to be improving with time. He adored her, sharing Julia's sense of humor, her spontaneity, and her love for music.

Julia's day seemed much like any other as well. She took care of her daughters, cooked meals, and tended to the house. After dinner she chatted with Bobby's mother before going to visit Mimi. The two sisters talked together until 9:30 PM, and then Julia left to catch the bus on Menlove Avenue. On most nights, Mimi typically walked Julia to the bus stop, which was just a few hundred yards away, but on this particular evening, she decided to stay at home. The two made plans to see each other the next day, and as Julia walked toward the street she saw John's friend Nigel Wally. Nigel was looking for John, and when he learned he was not at Mimi's, he walked with Julia toward the bus stop before turning toward his home. Menlove Avenue was divided by a hedge, and when Julia disappeared to the other side of the street, Nigel heard a horrible sound. Julia had been struck by car driven at a high speed by an off-duty police officer. Nigel ran immediately to Julia's side, as did Mimi, who heard the crash from her kitchen. Mimi rode with Julia in the ambulance to the Sefton General Hospital, but she knew there was no hope for her sister's recovery. Julia was pronounced dead on arrival. She was 44 years of age.

When Mimi arrived at the hospital, she immediately thought of John and tried to reach him by telephone so that he did not hear of the tragedy from a police officer, but she could not reach him in time. A police officer had already knocked on the door at Julia's home and delivered the unthinkable news. John and Bobby went immediately by taxi to the hospital. When they arrived, John could not bring himself to see his mother. He was devastated and never recovered from this loss, and the pain over Julia's death remained with him throughout his lifetime. The funeral was held a few days later at the Allerton Cemetery in Liverpool, but there would be no closure or solace for John. He later reflected, "It was the worst thing that ever happened to me. We'd caught up so much, me and Julia, in just a few years. We could communicate. We got on. She was great."[13]

Although the police officer responsible for Julia's death had only a learner's permit and should not have been driving alone, no charges were pressed against him.[14] He was briefly suspended from duty and later resigned to take a position as a postman. In a strange twist, years later, this same man delivered mail to the Forthlin Road, Allerton, where Paul McCartney lived.[15]

After Julia's death, Bobby Dykins was overcome with grief and overwhelmed by the responsibilities he faced as a single father. Bobby realized that he was not able to raise his daughters on his own, and he turned to Julia's sisters for help. John's half sisters, Jacqueline and Julia, were sent first to live with Mater and Uncle Bert in Edinburgh, and then to Harrie's in Woolton, where they were raised. Bobby moved into a home nearby Harrie's, providing her with money for their care. The girls visited him often, and they all remained in contact with John. Bobby even helped him to find a part-time job during his summer vacation at the Bear's Paw restaurant where Dykins was a manager.[16]

Alf, who was still legally married to Julia, learned of her death when his brother sent him the newspaper clipping about the accident. Since Alf was technically considered to be Julia's next of kin, he was automatically heir to her estate. Alf went to the solicitor's office in Liverpool shortly after Christmas in 1958 where he signed over his rights to Julia's possessions to John. Alf made no attempt to contact his son.

John was on his own to grieve privately and adjust to life without his free-spirited mother, publicly maintaining the stiff upper lip that was the norm in Britain in those days.[17] John's friends were not sure what to say to him, and his aunts kept their pain and loss to themselves as much as possible. Mimi, who had seen Julia nearly every day in the years before her death, fought back her tears for a long time after the tragedy. When John noticed, he would hug her and tell her not to worry, that he loved her.[18] The only friend who would come close to understanding John's loss and pain was Paul McCartney.

FRIENDSHIPS AND ROMANCE

During John's first year at art school, his friend Bill Harry introduced him to Stuart Sutcliffe, arguably the school's most talented student. The two soon forged what would become a very close friendship. The boys were the same age, but Stu was a year ahead of John in art school and a bit more independent. Stu had his own flat with his friend Rod Murray on Percy Street, and he often worked on his art in his flat rather than at the school. As Stu and John became closer friends, John began to stay at Stu's place, sometimes sleeping in a satin-lined coffin Stu installed in the flat, a reflection of their sense of humor.[19]

Stu was a serious and prolific artist, and John respected his accomplishments. One of Stu's paintings hung in John Moores's exhibition at the Walker Art Gallery in Liverpool, an achievement John particularly admired. Whereas Stu was intellectual and purposeful, John was intuitive and impulsive. A deep bond grew between the two. Stu often praised John for his wit and technique, and John valued Stu's compliments a great deal.

John learned much about art through his conversations and interactions with Stu, Bill, and Rod. Stu introduced John to Dadaism, a movement that involved rejection of the prevailing standards of art in the early 20th century. All four boys were avid readers, and they spent a great deal of time discussing and debating philosophical questions about the purpose and nature of human life. They all shared a keen interest in the uniqueness of Liverpool, and they decided to form a group called the Dissenters to celebrate and preserve this uniqueness through art, writing, and music.[20]

During John's second year of art school, he began a relationship with a woman named Thelma Pickles. Thelma and John shared a certain hostility toward the world, in part because of the problems and heartache they experienced in their families. Thelma's father left when she was just 10 years old, and she was raised by her mother. John continued to make mean and sarcastic remarks to people, including Thelma. Their relationship was stormy and short-lived.

Soon after John and Thelma broke up, John began a lettering class where he noticed a young art student named Cynthia Powell. She was from the middle-class suburbs in Hoylake, an area considered to be bourgeois. Cynthia's dream was to become an art teacher, and she was a diligent and conscientious student. Cynthia was initially frightened of John and his sharp tongue. When she walked into the classroom, John sarcastically admonished the others, "No dirty jokes, please—it's Cynthia."[21] John typically showed up for lettering class with no equipment, instead borrowing pencils or brushes from Cynthia. Cynthia was surprised that John was in a lettering class, knowing the painstaking work this involved, but she later learned that he was assigned to the class when the other art teachers refused to accept him into their classes.[22] John continued his antics, spending most of his time fooling around and making the class burst into laughter.

Although Cynthia was engaged to be married to another man, something attracted her to John. When she began her second year of school, she changed her hairstyle and clothing to be more fashionable and she even got rid of her eyeglasses, which presented her with endless problems, including sometimes missing her bus stop because she could not read the signs.[23] But her more stylish looks did not necessarily give her confidence against John's incessant teasing. While his first sarcastic remarks made Cynthia retreat from the classroom in embarrassment, Cynthia soon became enthralled by John's rebellious attitude and confident manner, and she looked forward to seeing him in class.[24]

John typically showed up for class with his guitar on his back, and he sometimes played for the students during class time. One day he played the popular tune "Ain't She Sweet," and he stared intently at Cynthia as he sang, causing her to blush and make an excuse to leave the room.[25] She realized at that moment that she had fallen for him, and wondered if perhaps he was interested in her as well. Shortly thereafter, John and Cynthia danced together to a Chuck Berry tune at a lunchtime celebration to mark the end of the 1958 winter term, and he asked her to go out with him. Caught off guard by his question, Cynthia replied that she was engaged to someone in Hoylake, and John snapped back by saying, "I didn't ask you to f***ing marry me, did I?"[26] Cynthia was sure she must have blown her chances to be with John, but before the party ended, John invited Cynthia and her friend Phyllis to join him and his friends at a popular nearby pub called Ye Cracke. Cynthia and John spent the afternoon at the pub, but he paid little attention to her while they were there. When she started to leave, he invited her to stay longer. They had a few drinks together and then went to Stu's flat on Percy Street. Here Cynthia told him that she was no longer engaged, and John confessed that he had been interested in her all term. John began to call her "Cyn," and what may have appeared to others to be an unlikely romance between a nice middle-class girl and a tough-acting guitar player began.

Soon John and Cynthia were spending all their spare time together, sometimes skipping classes in the afternoon to cross the Mersey River to New Brighton, where there was a funfair by the sea. John learned that Cynthia had lost her father to lung cancer a year earlier, and he understood the pain losing a parent must have brought to her. John became jealous of any boy who spoke with Cynthia, and at times he became angry with her, throwing tantrums and subjecting her to verbal abuse until she complied with his wishes.[27] At other times he was very romantic and loving toward her, writing her poems and drawing her pictures. Cynthia later recalled that their relationship was neither easy nor comfortable:

> There was an air of danger about John and he could terrify me. I lived on a knife edge. Not only was he passionately jealous but he could turn on me in an instant, belittling or berating me, shooting accusations, cutting remarks or acid wisecracks at me that left me hurt, frustrated and in tears.[28]

While John seemed to dare Cynthia to leave him, and while others advised her to do so,[29] she never did. Instead, she stayed quietly by his side, adhering to the compliant norms for women in 1950s Britain. Cynthia even changed her appearance to please John, dying her hair and wearing tight skirts and fishnet stockings to resemble John's favorite actress, Brigitte Bardot.[30]

END OF THE QUARRYMEN

As John's relationship with Cynthia grew, he continued to write music and play guitar every chance he could. Cynthia often listened to John, Paul, and George practice during lunch hour at art school. Finally it appeared the boys had a break. They were offered a much-needed gig playing at the opening of a new club called the Casbah in the West Derby suburb of Liverpool. The owner, Mona Best, opened the club in a cellar as a place for her son, Pete, to hang out with his friends. Ken Brown was on guitar, but the band had no drummer at the time. At the opening, the boys were introduced to Neil Aspinall, Pete's mother's boyfriend, and Mal Evans, men who would later become loyal road-ies for the Beatles. Mona liked what she heard, and the Quarrymen became regulars at the Casbah, sometimes playing to crowds that num-bered as many as 400 people. Each time they played, the boys earned 15 shillings each.[31]

Soon Pete Best decided he wanted to form his own group, and he purchased a drum set and recruited a friend named Ken Brown. The two formed a band called the Blackjacks, and they became the reg-ular gig at the Casbah, replacing the Quarrymen, who subsequently performed there only occasionally. Shortly after this, John, Paul, and George auditioned as Johnny and the Moondogs for Carroll Levis, who was known as the Starmaker.[32] But much to their disappointment, they failed miserably, primarily because they had no drummer. The Quarry-men seemed to be doomed, and the group officially disbanded in early 1959 after a gig at Bushman's Club in Prescott Road. They became drunk during intermission and the second set was terrible. Colin got into an argument with Paul and quit, and there seemed to be no point in continuing the group.

In 1960, John moved out of Mendips and into Stu's flat. Mimi was quite upset, and she even asked Cynthia, who she was not fond of, to persuade him to move back home.[33] Stu's place was known for its squalor. A July 24, 1960 issue of The People included it in an article called "The Beatnik Horror," which highlighted the unusual living conditions among young people. John is in the middle of the article's photo, lying on the floor in Stu's flat.[34] But Mimi did not need to worry too much. She still saw her nephew. John took his laundry to Mimi's because she agreed to wash his clothes. He also had meals with her on a fairly regular basis.

When Stu won a prestigious art award, which earned him £60, John convinced him to purchase a Hohner bass guitar rather than art sup-plies, and he invited him join his band. Bill Harry, while supportive of John and his music goals, felt Stu was making a mistake by spending so much time with music, particularly since he was such a talented visual artist.[35] But Stu could never say no to John. Stu practiced for hours on end, and he took lessons from a teacher named Dave May, but in spite of his effort Stu did not bring a lot of musical strength to the band. Even his teacher thought he was hopeless.[36] When Stu began to perform on stage, he often turned his back to the audience so that they could not see how little he was actually playing. John did not mind; he was just glad to have his friend as part of the group. Stu's presence seemed to bother Paul, however. Paul was more of a perfectionist, and Stu's playing may have been inadequate to him. Paul also may have been a bit jealous of Stu's relationship with John.[37]

As the Quarrymen ended, the boys decided they needed to make some changes if they were going to continue to perform. They decided to dress differently, wearing black jeans and polo neck shirts, and they completely dropped the old skiffle sounds to exclusively play the rock and roll tunes that were popular at the time. The boys decided they needed a name change to reflect their new image and sound, so they sat together with Cynthia at the Renshaw Hall bar, joking around with insect names primarily because John liked Buddy Holly and the Crickets. Finally John came up with the Beetles. This was the name of a gang in a Marlon Brando motorcycle romance film popular at the time, but biographer Philip Norman claimed this had no influence on the boys' choice of band names because the boys had never seen the film.[38] John changed the spelling to Beatles, which, when switched around in his usual language play, was les beat. Breaking with what was typical in those days, when band names had someone as the front man in the name for a band (for example, Buddy Holly and the Crickets), the group decided on the Silver Beatles.

Not too long after this, the Silver Beatles auditioned for Larry Parnes. Parnes had a reputation for discovering new talent and he was connected to many popular bands at the time. The Silver Beatles still had no drummer, and so someone from another group sat in with them, but it did not help them much. They failed the audition. Paul blamed Stu's poor playing.[39] Parnes was not able to send them on tour as backup for Billy Fury, which is what John was hoping would happen; however, he did send them on tour with a lesser-known singer named Johnny Gentle. George had to take time off work, and John and Stuart had to miss a week of school, which was not too much of a concern for John. Paul needed to convince his father that going on this short tour of Scotland would give him a much needed break before he took his A-level exams in a few weeks. Once their schedules were adjusted, the boys needed to find a drummer. They invited a Liverpool musician named Tommy Moore, and fortunately he agreed to join them. The Silver Beatles finally had what they considered to be their first big break.

NOTES

1. Philip Norman, *John Lennon: The Life* (New York: Harper Collins Publishers, 2008), p. 115.

2. Ibid., p. 127.

3. Ibid., p. 129.

4. Hunter Davies, *The Beatles* (New York: McGraw Hill Publishing, 1985), p. 57

5. Elizabeth Partridge, *John Lennon: All I Want Is the Truth* (New York: Viking Press, 2005), p. 50.

6. John Robertson, *The Art and Music of John Lennon* (New York: Carol Publishing Group, 1991), p. 4.

7. Albert Goldman, *The Lives of John Lennon* (New York: William Morrow and Company, 1988), p. 71. A Scouse accent indicated that a person was from a particular neighborhood in Liverpool, most often of the lower social class.

8. Partridge, p. 54.

9. Cynthia Lennon, *John* (New York: Crown Publishers, 2005), p. 33.

10. Partridge, p. 54.

11. Norman, p. 164.

12. The boys were given five copies of the disc, but only one survives and is in Paul McCartney's possession.

13. Norman, p. 146.

14. Ibid.

15. Ibid., p. 150.

16. Ibid.

17. Ibid., p. 151.

18. Ibid., p. 152.

19. Goldman, p. 84.

20. Norman, p. 136.
21. Partridge, p. 60.
22. Lennon, p. 18.
23. Ibid., p. 17.
24. Ibid., p. 18.
25. Ibid., p. 19.
26. Ibid., p. 21.
27. Ibid., p. 26.
28. Ibid., p. 27.
29. Partridge, p. 62.
30. Norman, p. 157.
31. Lennon, p. 33.
32. Ibid., p. 34.
33. Ibid., p. 47.
34. Goldman, p. 84.
35. Norman, p. 168.
36. Goldman, p. 85.
37. Lennon, p. 48.
38. Norman, p. 172.
39. Lennon, p. 49.

Chapter 3

THE BEATLES

Working as the backup band for Johnny Gentle gave the Beatles their first chance to tour the United Kingdom. The eight-day tour of seven towns across northeastern Scotland consisted of the Silver Beatles opening the act by playing six tunes, mostly from Little Richard's music. When they finished, Johnny Gentle joined them onstage to perform Ricky Nelson songs like "Mary Lou" and "Poor Little Fool." When Gentle finished, the Silver Beatles played six more tunes. They were paid 5 pounds per person, with the exception of Stu, since Larry Parnes did not want him on the tour. John refused to let the band play without his friend, and he convinced the others to pool their money so Stu could be paid.[1]

In spite of the boys' initial enthusiasm for the tour and their excitement at seeing their names on the posters, life on the road took its toll. The tour was poorly organized, they traveled in an old and uncomfortable van, and their expenses were barely covered. Tempers raged. John, Paul, and George were accustomed to arguing with each other, and none of them took their squabbles too seriously. Stu, however, was a different story. He was not used to their ways and as the newest member of the group, the boys often ganged up on him, telling him he could not eat with them or that he should go away.[2] Stu took them seriously.[3] So did drummer Tommy Moore, who was financially broke and quickly tired of John's beatnik attitude and ruthlessness toward others. Shortly after they returned to Liverpool, Tommy quit the band, earning himself the distinction of being the only person to ever quit the Beatles. He later recalled: "I'd had a bellyful of Lennon . . . he could be a bloody nasty guy."[4]

Needless to say, the boys returned to Liverpool exhausted and broke, but they ended the tour a much better band after performing together for hours on the road. The tour gave John a glimpse of what his future could be. As girls crowded around Johnny Gentle seeking autographs during the tour, John yelled out, "That'll be us some day, Johnny."[5] Gentle later recalled that John Lennon knew he was going places, even in those early days and he saw a spark in him. Gentle advised the band to go to London.

After returning from Scotland, John failed his art school exams and was expelled. He did not seem to be too concerned, and years later he admitted having no regrets. He summed up his school experiences by saying:

> I've been proved right. They were wrong and I was right. They're all still there, aren't they, so *they* must be the failures . . . [Teachers] should give you time to develop, encourage what you're interested in. I was always interested in art . . . but no one took any interest. . . . All they were interested in was neatness. I was never neat, I used to mix all the colors together.[6]

John realized he wished to spend his time playing music. The band had regular work in Liverpool, which is what he wanted, and in August 1960, their next big break came.

GERMANY

Promoter Allan Williams, who had a club in Liverpool, arranged for the Beatles to play a six-week gig in Hamburg, Germany. They had to quickly find a drummer and decided to ask Pete Best, who was looking for a new group after his band, the Blackjacks, broke up. Fortunately, he agreed. Now the band was complete.

On August 15, 1960, the boys loaded into Allan Williams's van and took off for Hamburg, Germany, where they played for two months at the Club Indra, and then at the Kaiserkeller. These venues were different than what any the band members had experienced in Liverpool or Scotland. Both were located in Reeperbahn in the St. Pauli district of Hamburg, a rough neighborhood with many nightclubs, strip joints, and bars serving alcohol at all hours of the day. Due in large part to the American military's occupation of West Germany, these clubs began to play rock and roll music, mostly on jukeboxes. But Bruno Koschmider, who owned the Club Indra and the Kaiserkeller, decided to have live music at his establishments. Sailors on shore leave from all around the world, as well as British and American NATO forces, frequented the Club Indra and the Kaiserkeller. Many of the clientele were short-tempered, and fights broke out frequently.

When the boys arrived at the Club Indra, they soon realized the gig that preceded them was a girlie show, and initially the audience was not too friendly toward them. But soon they learned to play for the crowd, offering a performance, not just music. In England, the boys were accustomed to playing one-hour sets, but in Hamburg, they were expected to play as much as six to eight hours each night. The club's owner yelled at them to "Mach Schau!"[7] (Make show!), so John, Paul, and George danced and joked around on the stage, cavorting in exaggerated ways that made the audience laugh. John was perhaps the most daring, calling the audience members names, including Nazis and Krauts, which was no small matter considering that World War II had ended just 15 years earlier. The Beatles smoked and ate while they were on stage, and the audience showed their appreciation by sending them drinks and giving them nicknames: crazy Beatles, or later, because of their hairstyles, mushroom heads.[8] Soon their audience grew to fill the club.

The music the boys played in Hamburg ranged from Elvis, Buddy Holly, and other American artists to country music, skiffle, traditional standards, and show tunes, including "Somewhere Over the Rainbow."[9] Because they had to play sets that lasted an hour and a half, they expanded their repertoire and they learned to jam, stretching out songs with impromptu riffs and improvisations. To keep their energy levels high, the boys began to take pills called prellies.[10]

While in Germany, the Beatles stayed in a dingy living quarter in an old cinema called the Bambi. They had to use the public restrooms in the cinema, washing up in the sinks because they had no shower or bathtub to use. John complained about these conditions in his letters to Cynthia, but she knew John well and could tell that he was really enjoying the experience overall.[11] When he was not on the stage, John spent his free time reading newspapers, walking around the city, and when the mood struck him he occasionally shoplifted.[12]

When they were not on stage, the boys hung out with a group of art students known as "Exis" (existentialists). Art students did not typically frequent this area of Hamburg, but Klaus Voorman inadvertently wandered in the club one evening after he heard the band from the street.[13] He was intrigued with their performance and invited his photographer girlfriend Astrid Kirchherr and other friends, including Jurgen Vollmer to join him. Soon they were the Beatles' biggest fans, and they went to the club almost every night. Since none of the Beatles could speak German and few of Voorman's friends spoke English, they sometimes struggled to communicate. George was perhaps the most patient, speaking slowly so that he could be understood.[14]

The boys were completely taken with Astrid. She was stylish and sophisticated, and she had a very avant-garde lifestyle.[15] They visited her home for sandwiches and tea and were fascinated with her room, which was decorated black and white. Astrid convinced the boys to let her take photographs of them. She shot some of the most famous photos of the Beatles during their early years, and her style, which used shadows and interesting locations like a railroad yard, influenced many photographers who followed her.

John faithfully wrote long, often rambling and detailed letters to Cynthia when was he was in Germany. He told of their performances and all the things they were doing, and he included little drawings and poems with the letters. Cynthia missed John terribly and was always pleased to hear from him; however, when he began writing about Astrid in almost every letter to Cynthia, she began to feel some pangs of jealousy. She soon learned that her worries were unfounded. Astrid had fallen in love with Stu. Astrid broke off her relationship with Klaus, and became engaged to Stu, who moved in with Astrid and her mother.

The boys began to explore other work possibilities in Hamburg, including one at a club called the Top Ten, where they heard Tony Sheridan play a few times. Sheridan and his band, the Jets, arrived at the Reeperbahn from London a few months ahead of the Beatles. The Beatles jammed a few times with Sheridan; however, this violated their contract with Kaiserkeller owner Bruno Koschmider, who was not happy to hear of their plans to move to the Top Ten. Soon after, the police were alerted that George Harrison was only 17 years of age and did not have a work permit or resident's permit. He was ordered to leave the country immediately. A few days later, Paul and Pete accidentally knocked over a candle at the Bambi theater, which started a small fire. Koschmider was again furious, and the two were ordered to leave. Once they departed, John was told that his work permit was being revoked, so he too had to head back to Liverpool. He had very little money in hand, even though he made a decent salary in the Hamburg clubs.[16] Stu soon followed, reluctantly leaving Astrid behind.

RETURN TO LIVERPOOL

John was eager to see Cynthia when he returned to Liverpool and to have her share in his experiences, including the new fashion sense he learned from Astrid, so as soon as he returned home, he took her shopping to buy a new leather coat that was similar in style to those being worn in Germany. After reuniting with Cynthia, John went to visit Mimi. He took Cynthia, who was wearing his new coat, along with him to Mendips. They stopped at a market on the way to buy a cooked chicken for Mimi and their afternoon tea. John thought this would be a nice gesture for his aunt, but when Mimi opened the door and saw the chicken and Cynthia's new coat, she lashed out at John by saying, "Do you think you can butter me up with a chicken when you've spent all your money on [Cynthia's coat]? Get out."[17] John took Cynthia's arm and left immediately, commenting on his way out that all Mimi cared about was money and cats. He was obviously hurt by her outburst and rage.[18]

Cynthia later observed that the image Mimi portrayed in interviews about her life with John were not accurate; Cynthia's perspective was that Mimi could never be pleased and that she often "battered away at John's self-confidence and left him angry and hurt."[19] There was no sense of mutual admiration between the two women. Mimi saw Cynthia as a rival for John's affection and attention.[20]

For a few weeks after returning from Hamburg, the Beatles did not get together. George and Paul found jobs because they were uncertain about the future of the band. John eventually returned to live at Mendips, harboring doubts about whether he would be successful as a musician. John did not believe he was a good singer, and certainly he did not sound like other famous musicians at the time. He also did not have much confidence in his guitar playing. John's cocky attitude and sarcastic wit made him seem like a tough guy on the surface, but those who were close to him realized this was not the case.[21] John continued to learn everything he could about music from people around him, including Tony Sheridan, and he continued to create music and try new sounds on his guitar, but in the days after his return from Hamburg, he did some soul searching as he tried to determine whether playing music really was for him. In the end he came to the conclusion that it was.

When the Beatles finally did reunite, they renewed their commitment to one another and to continuing the band. Their first gig in Liverpool was a return to the Casbah, where fans screamed with excitement over the changes and improvements in the Beatles. The boys' time in Germany had certainly influenced them—they were better musicians, they wore leather coats and had a style that was different than other Liverpool bands, and they performed for the crowd with the energy and humor that captivated audiences in Hamburg. After the Casbah, they performed at the Litherland Town Hall, the largest venue they had ever played. Again, the hall was packed with screaming fans. The Beatles let it all out just like they had learned to do in Germany. The crowd went wild.

The Beatles quickly became a huge hit in Liverpool. Fans loved them and crowded into their performances, and girls went wild just to see the Beatles on stage. Off stage, however, things started to get rough for the boys. Teddy Boys, jealous of their girlfriends' obsessions with the Beatles, would sometimes wait outside the show when it ended. As equipment was being loaded in the vans, the Teds tried to fight with the boys. They soon learned how to make a quick escape from a concert venue, something that would be invaluable in the years to come.

THE CAVERN

One of the more popular clubs in Liverpool was The Cavern, a dark and damp basement on Mathew Street, close to the city center in the fruit market area of Liverpool. The ventilation and acoustics were horrible, but it was one of the most popular places for young people to gather, especially when they learned the Beatles would be there. The boys played a lunch gig at The Cavern on Tuesday February 9, 1961, the first of what would eventually be 292 lunchtime and evening performances in this venue. Bob Wooler served as announcer and introduced the Beatles to the crowd each time they performed.

The Beatles were obviously different than any other rock band at that time. They had no featured front man, and while John was clearly acknowledged as the band's leader, he and Paul shared a chemistry and tension on stage that thrilled the audiences. If something went wrong on stage, the boys hammed it up. If an amp shorted out, they asked the crowd to join in singing a rousing chorus of "Coming Round the Mountain."[22] John continued to squint on stage, often looking down his nose at the audience because he still refused to wear glasses. He frequently taunted the crowd, particularly those who showed up in suits, and he sang many songs in a joking, mocking manner, sometimes adopting accents and imitating voices of other people. Paul was friendlier toward the audience than John was, wooing the girls with his smile and big brown eyes, but he joked around on stage too. Since they played over the lunch hour, the boys often ate their lunch as they performed. George, Stu, and Pete, who were all quiet and more serious, tended to remain in the background.

As they gained more confidence with the crowd, John and Paul began to include their original music in the line-up. The first was "Like Dreamers Do," and it was a hit. Given this success, they added two other new tunes—"Hold Me Tight" and "Love Me Do"—to their set.[23] The boys interspersed these numbers with American songs, including Larry Williams's "Slow Down," the Marvelettes' "Please Mister Postman," and Carl Perkins's "Glad All Over." They did not seem to mind if the songs were written to be sung by girls for boys; in fact, they did not care to change the lyrics to make the songs more gender accurate.

Family and friends of the Beatles stopped by to hear their performances at The Cavern. Paul and George's parents visited most often. Jim Mc-Cartney was a single working father now that he was widowed, and his son's fame, at least in the Liverpool area, did not diminish the practical needs he had to meet to keep his family together. He usually left meat he picked up for dinner in Paul's dressing room along with instructions about how to get dinner started later that day. George's mother was perhaps the most devoted fan among the boys' parents, and she often took family and friends to see their shows.[24] Mimi went to The Cavern only once, teetering down the steep stairs into the noisy darkness. She grew angry as she watched John cavorting about on the stage, and she did not stay very long.[25] Mimi thought that the Beatles were going nowhere that and John should get a decent job, and she told him so.

John's girlfriend, Cynthia, was a regular at The Cavern, but she quickly learned to keep her presence discreet. If she was noticed, jealous Beatles fans sometimes accosted her, which meant she needed to avoid the ladies' restroom during breaks in the band's show.[26]

Although the Beatles had a growing and loyal fan base in Liverpool, they still yearned for Hamburg. They made plans for a return visit in March of 1961. This trip was much like the first. The boys played long gigs in the club each night to raucous crowds, taking prellies to keep their energy levels high.

A few weeks after they left Liverpool, John decided to have Cynthia join him in Hamburg. She traveled there with Paul's girlfriend, Dot Rhone. John spent his free time showing Cynthia around the city, and then he returned to the stage each evening with the other members of the band. Cynthia went to the club every night with Astrid and Dot to see the boys' performances. Cynthia later remembered that these were some of the happiest and most carefree times she had with John.[27] Paul was likewise glad to see Dot, and he asked her to marry him. John suggested to Cynthia that they should become engaged too, but they waited.

As their time in Hamburg came to a close, the boys were feeling quite good about the work they had accomplished. In addition to the success of their show at the club, the Beatles had their first official recording, as "the Beat Boys," playing backup singers for Tony Sheridan on a song called "My Bonnie." But their happiness with their success in Hamburg was tempered a bit, at least for John. Stu did not return with them to Liverpool. Paul gave Stu a difficult time for not practicing enough and being a poor musician, even though John was not concerned about this. Stu was more interested in painting, and this was how he wanted to spend his time. He made plans to return to art school and marry Astrid. The boys could not be too bitter about this; they all adored Astrid. She left an indelible mark on the band, and not just because they admired her in so many ways. It was Astrid who encouraged Stu to comb his Teddy Boy hairstyle forward to frame his face. Although the other Beatles laughed at him at first, they soon followed his lead, creating the mop-top haircut that would become a trademark part of their image. Astrid also had an influence on some of their clothing styles. In the end, Stu's departure was not a big problem for the band musically, but it was a loss for John personally. Stu was his best friend.

When the boys returned from Hamburg, John began to publish his writing in a local newspaper called *Mersey Beat*, edited by his college friend Bill Harry. John's first story, titled "Being a Short Diversion on the Dubious Origins of the Beatles," told how the Beatles first got together. The piece was written in a fairytale style with humor that was typical of John's writing but was not particularly commonplace for that time. He began, "Once upon a time there were three little boys called John, George, and Paul, by name christened. They decided to get together because they were the getting together type."[28] John mentioned Stu in the story as well, with reference to the fact that he couldn't play, and he wrote about their ongoing struggles to retain a percussionist. Notably, John addressed a common question posed to the boys about how they came up with the band's name, creating a story that was oft-repeated in the years to come:

Many people ask what are Beatles? Why Beatles? Ugh, Beatles, how did the name arrive? So we will tell you. It came in a vision—a man appeared on a flaming pie and said unto them, "From this day on, you are Beatles with an A." Thank you Mister Man, they said, thanking him.[29]

John was thrilled when he saw his writing in print, and he soon offered *Mersey Beat* more of his drawings, poetry, and stories.[30]

When John turned 21, Mater and Uncle Bert gave him 100 pounds, quite a generous gift. John was not particularly happy about turning 21. He thought he was old, at least too old to be pursuing music professionally, and he considered studying art again.[31] Many of the American groups at the time seemed to have much younger band members. Needing some time away, John decided to take Paul to Paris for two weeks with his birthday money. They reconnected with their German friend Jurgen Vollmer and spent their time hanging out at cafes, visiting art museums, and taking in the local music scene. When John's money ran out, the two returned to Liverpool only to find George Harrison and Pete Best ready to quit the band. Several of their promoters were angry because John and Paul never told anyone they were leaving. They were lectured on the importance of honoring their engagements.[32]

NEW MANAGEMENT

Shortly after John and Paul returned from Paris, a young man walked into the Northern England Music and Electric Industries (NEMS) record shop in Liverpool and asked for a copy of the "My Bonnie" album the Beatles had recorded in Hamburg. The record store manager, Brian Epstein, who preferred classical music over the beat scene that was storming Liverpool, had never heard of the album or of the Beatles. Since his business strategy was to make any album available to his customers, Epstein made it a point to learn more about them, and on October 28, 1961, Epstein began to sell "Tony Sheridan and the Beat Brothers" on 45 rpm. To his surprise, it outsold albums by Elvis and Cliff Richard.

This piqued Epstein's curiosity about this band, which he originally thought was German, and on November 9, 1961, he went to The Cavern to hear the Beatles perform. He was somewhat surprised by their on-stage antics as they cracked jokes with the audience and turned their backs on the crowd as they sang and ate on stage, but it was clear the young crowd adored them.

Brian was soon taken with the group and decided he wanted to become their manager. Brian's proposal came at an opportune time. The Beatles had become more confident with their business endeavors. They had a fan club, and their management had evolved into a shared activity among the boys, Mona Best at the Casbah club, Neil Aspinall, their faithful driver, and Ray McFall, who owned The Cavern. Bill Harry and Bob Wooler, both promoters knowledgeable of the Liverpool music scene, helped them stay onstage in the Liverpool area, and Sam Leach tried to get them bookings in London.[33] But there was a growing sense that if they were going to take the band to the next level, they needed a manager who could promote them outside of Liverpool.

Brian Epstein invited the boys to his office on December 3 to discuss the terms under which he would manage them. Bob Wooler, who John referred to as his father during the meeting, joined them. John was impressed with Brian, but the other Beatles were not convinced he was the right person to manage them. Brian came from a wealthy family, and they were distrustful of his motives. Yet the Beatles were eager to take their touring to the next level, and although Epstein had no previous experience managing bands, he was a well-established, excellent businessman and he had a lot of ideas about how to promote the Beatles.

A week after they met in Epstein's office, the Beatles agreed to the partnership. John was the only one old enough to legally sign the contract, so Brian had to follow up with the McCartney, Harrison, and Best families to have the boys' guardians provide legal consent. As a courtesy, Brian also visited with Mimi at Mendips. For once she was impressed with someone John brought home and gave her blessings. In the end, John and the other boys' guardians all signed the contract, which gave Brian 25 percent of their earnings.

Brian set to work right away to change the boys' image, shaping them into a more clean-cut looking group. His other top priority was to find them a recording contract. Around Christmas, Brian convinced Mike Smith from Decca records to come to Liverpool to hear the boys perform. It was unheard of at that time for a top executive to travel so far to hear a band play, but Smith made the trip.[34] He was impressed with what he heard and invited the boys to London for an audition. Neil Aspinall, now officially the band's road manager, drove the boys through a snow storm to London for the audition on New Years Eve.

The next day, the Beatles went to the studio to play, but they were quite nervous. Paul's voice cracked a good deal, and none performed at their best. The boys heard nothing from Decca for nearly three months, and when they did, the news was not good—Decca was not interested. They were told that their sound was not good and that guitar bands were on their way out. The boys were disappointed, of course, but Brian persevered. He continued to travel back and forth to London, attempting to find a record contract.

HAMBURG, AGAIN

In April, the Beatles embarked on their third trip to Hamburg. Their earnings were doubled from just a year earlier, and so the boys decided to fly from Rengway Airport in Manchester rather than ride in a van. This time they were set to play the Star-Club, which was promised to be the world's greatest rock club.

The boys were looking forward to a reunion with Stu, Astrid, and their other German friends. Stu and Astrid planned to meet the Beatles at the airport, but when the boys disembarked in Germany, they were surprised to see that Astrid was the only one there. As they greeted her, Astrid shared unexpected and devastating news: Stu had died the day before the boys arrived, the result of a blood clot on his brain. He had a small brain tumor near a lesion on his brain, which his mother thought was the result of a fight.

John's initial reaction to Astrid's news was similar to when he learned his Uncle George had died—he broke into hysterical laughter. John adored Stu and deep down he was devastated by this loss, and some speculated he felt guilty about it. Some members of Stu's family believed John once fought Stu in a fit of rage when they were in Hamburg on a previous visit, and that he punched Stu to the ground and kicked him in the head with pointed cowboy boots. Stu's family later claimed Stu told them about this incident during what would be his final trip home to Liverpool, but they kept this to themselves, wishing for Stu to be known for his creative work and not as a "footnote to the Beatles."[35] Paul supposedly witnessed the event,[36] but neither he nor Astrid seemed to remember this alleged attack, and others who were questioned felt John could never have lashed out so violently against Stu, particularly since he always seemed to be protective of him.[37]

In spite of whether this fight happened and whether it contributed directly to Stu's death, John suffered greatly over the loss of his dear friend. Although John did not attend Stu's funeral and said little publicly about his friend's death, Astrid later wrote to Stu's mother to tell her that John grieved deeply and had asked why he couldn't go to heaven in Stu's place.[38] She described John's room in the letter, explaining that he had photos and papers from Stu hung on his walls. John seemed to harbor anger of the fact that the people he loved the most died, first his mother and then Stu.[39] John was able to put his own feelings aside to help Astrid through this difficult time, encouraging her to continue to live and insisting that she come to see the Beatles' shows.[40]

Although the boys were experiencing a great deal of shock and grief over Stu's death, the show had to go on, and the Beatles opened at the Star-Club to great reviews. John performed with an intensity on stage that now seemed to remain with him all the time. It was difficult to know how much of his behavior could be attributed to grief, and how much was due to the difficult schedule they maintained. John drank heavily, took pills, and spent time with his Hamburg girlfriend Bettina Derlien, one of the bartenders at the club.[41]

Shortly after the Hamburg opening, Brian Epstein secured a recording session for the Beatles with the record label EMI. They returned from Hamburg in early June, and auditioned for producer George Martin a few days later. For the audition, they played a mixture of well-known tunes and their original pieces. It took two months for them to hear the outcome of the audition, but this time the news was good. George Martin wanted them to sign a contract with Parlaphone Records, a company that was part of EMI. Needless to say, the boys were ecstatic. John kept shouting to Cynthia, "This is it, Cyn, this is it, we're going to be making records. We're famous!"[42]

The boys celebrated when they heard word about the record deal, with the exception of Pete Best. George Martin indicated that Pete was not strong enough to play on the recording, and he wanted to hire a session drummer in his place.[43] John, Paul, and George understood Martin's concerns, and they decided that it was time for Pete to leave the band. John, Paul, and George asked Brian to fire Pete just before the EMI recording got underway. Cutting Pete from the band was not handled with great finesse, and although Pete and John had been friends for four years, John avoided him.[44]

Once Pete was cut from the band, the remaining Beatles had two immediate problems: they needed to face fans who were not happy that Pete was gone, and they needed to find another drummer. They could not do too much about the fans, but they had to act quickly to find a drummer. They knew of one possibility—Ringo Starr.

FINDING RINGO

Ringo (born Richard Starkey) grew up in Dingle, a poor neighborhood in Liverpool. Ringo's parents divorced when he was three years old, and his mother raised him on her own, working as a bar maid. They never had much money. Ringo was very sickly as a child, which caused him to miss years of school. When he was six years of age, he had appendicitis followed by a serious case of peritonitis. He had two operations and ended up staying in the hospital for a year. At the time, people believed that parent visits to the hospital only upset the children, and so his mother could only look in on Ringo when he was asleep. He never knew she was there.

After a year in the hospital, Ringo was quite behind with his schoolwork, and he struggled to catch up. Then he became sick again when he was 13 years old. He suffered from pleurisy and was hospitalized for nearly two years. When Ringo was discharged, he realized there was little chance of him finishing school, so he began to learn a trade, hoping that would lead to a decent living. Then the skiffle craze hit Liverpool and Ringo joined a band.

The Beatles first met Ringo when he played for Rory Storm and the Hurricanes in Hamburg. Ringo sat in with the Beatles a few times when Pete was sick, so he was familiar with their music and style. John, Paul, and George got along well with the amiable Ringo, and they decided to ask him to join the Beatles. Brian called to ask Ringo to join the band on a Wednesday, and Ringo agreed since the Beatles would pay more per week (£25) than any other group that made him an offer.[45] Ringo officially debuted with the Beatles at an out-of-town gig, but eventually the band had to return to Liverpool. They knew this would not be easy. Crowds waiting to enter The Cavern on Mathew Street were still loyal to Pete, and they chanted, "Pete forever, Ringo never" or "Pete is Best."[46]

MARRYING CYNTHIA

In early August, Cynthia told John she was expecting a baby. Although this was a surprise to them, the couple decided they should marry. Mimi did everything she possibly could to talk John out of the marriage, even threatening to never speak to him again, but in the end, she gave John £10 for a wedding ring since he had no money. She later described John on the night before his wedding as having wandered through the house at Mendips and eventually crying in the kitchen.[47]

Cynthia reported a different story. She explained that although John went pale and was at first silent when Cynthia told him about the baby, he rallied and told her that they would be married. According to Cynthia, John said, "I love you and I'm not going to leave you now."[48]

John's conviction that the two should wed was riddled with fear about the consequences for the Beatles. Brian cautioned the boys repeatedly that fans would not be so accepting if one of them had a steady girlfriend, let alone a wife. He was worried about the impact on their fans if John became a husband, let alone a father. In spite of this, on August 23, 1962, John and Cynthia were married at the Mount Pleasant register office in Liverpool. Brian drove Cynthia to the ceremony. George and Paul, wearing black, attended to show their support for John, and Cynthia's brother Tony, and his wife, Marjorie, were there for Cynthia, whose mother had recently moved to Canada and could not return for the ceremony. Mimi refused to attend.[49]

Cynthia described the ceremony as comic. When the registrar began to recite the vows, the sound of a pneumatic drill from a nearby construction site overwhelmed the room. John and Cynthia had to shout in order to be heard. George also got in on the fun. When the registrar asked for the groom to step forward, George did so as a joke. When the ceremony was over, Brian suggested they have lunch at the nearby Reece's café. He treated them to soup, chicken, and trifle. Little known to John and Cynthia at the time, their wedding was remarkably similar to Julia and Alfred's so many years before: they were wed at the same office and ate lunch at the same café after the ceremony ended.

Brian allowed John and Cynthia to use his flat on Faulkner Street after they were married. On their wedding night, John went to Chester to perform with the Beatles in a gig that had been scheduled weeks before the two decided to get married, while Cynthia arranged their few belongings in their new home. Although John remained quite busy with the Beatles, Cynthia described their first weeks of marriage as happy ones, although she was often quite lonely. John often surprised her with flowers and gifts, including a new coffee table he purchased at Harrods.[50] Their marriage and pregnancy remained a secret, with the exception of the couple's closest friends and family.

Shortly after John married Cynthia, the Beatles went to London to record their first single, "Love Me Do," working with George Martin at Parlaphone Records. Martin asked Paul to sing lead, and he asked John to play his harmonica to add a more bluesy feel to the piece. "PS I Love You" was recorded for the B-side of the single.

Martin had specific ideas about the recording, which included bringing in a session drummer rather than using Ringo. Of course Ringo was devastated, but the boys soon learned to trust Martin. Martin was a classical musician educated at London's Guildhall School of Music, where he had studied piano and oboe, and while he was not initially well-versed with rock music, his understandings of music and his skills brought a professionalism to the Beatles' sound that the group needed. He was soon a critical element of the Beatles' creative process, and later was sometimes referred to as the fifth Beatle. Martin was impressed with the boys, and as they finished recording this first single, he pressed the intercom button to speak to the boys in the studio, telling them, "Gentlemen, you've just made your first number one record!"[51]

Three weeks after its release, "Love Me Do" reached number 49 on the British charts, a disappointment for the Beatles. But things would soon change. Little Richard toured the United Kingdom with Sam Cooke in October, and Brian arranged for the boys to perform second on the bill when the show played one night in New Brighton. This was a huge thrill for John, who was so influenced by Little Richard's music during his schooldays. The show was a big success, and Brian arranged for Little Richard to perform in Liverpool on October 28, the same day the Cuban Missile Crisis was resolved. Spirits among the fans were high and everyone enjoyed the performance.

John continued to be very busy with the Beatles, and the fact that he was married and expecting a child did not seem to have an impact on him. Life in Brian's flat was a bit difficult for Cynthia. The bathroom was separate from the apartment, she was incredibly lonely, and the neighborhood was a bit rough. Mimi offered to have John and Cynthia move into the ground floor at Mendips, and Cynthia, who was suffering from being alone nearly all the time, welcomed the offer. Mimi's generosity did not go unnoticed. As John's personal wealth grew, he looked after Mimi, paying off the mortgage on Mendips and buying her furniture and other niceties for her home.[52]

The Beatles returned once again to Hamburg as "Love Me Do" slowly climbed the charts. John was not too excited to return to Germany given the success the Beatles were realizing in England, but Brian insisted they must honor their contract.[53] After their obligations were fulfilled, John and the Beatles went to London to record their second single "Please Please Me," which would be released after the new year. John wrote the song in part to emulate some of Roy Orbison's style. After the recording session ended, they played for their fifth time in Hamburg with performances that ran from December 18 to 31, 1962.

TOURING THE UNITED KINGDOM

In February, the Beatles went on their first national tour of Britain, backing singer Helen Shapiro. When they were on tour, "Please Please Me" climbed to number one after a slow and somewhat erratic ascent through the charts. The song started to reach a wider audience after a January 19 Beatles performance on the popular British television show *Thank Your Lucky Stars*. The show serendipitously aired during a snowstorm, and the audience of teenage viewers was quite large that evening.[54] Soon after, young people called radio stations to request the song.

The Beatles next tour began in March with musicians Chris Montez and Tommy Roe. The Beatles were third on the bill but clearly growing in popularity. Neil Aspinall diligently helped to set up and test their equipment at the different venues, but the work was nearly impossible for one person to do, particularly as the fans became more and more aggressive. The boys decided to ask Mal Evans, the bouncer from The Cavern, to join them on tour.[55]

The Beatles recorded their first LP, also titled *Please Please Me*, in a marathon 11-hour session. The session was kept to one day in part

because EMI did not wish to spend a great deal of money on the recording, and the Beatles' touring schedule made it difficult to arrange the
studio time. Fortunately producer George Martin was experienced and
creative. He decided to record the Beatles performing the best pieces
from their Cavern days as though they were in a live performance.[56]
It was a long session, and the last song they recorded was "Twist and
Shout." John knew he couldn't do too many takes of the song because
his voice was shot, and he later said that all he could at that point in
the recording process was scream. They played four original Lennon-
McCartney tunes, and then filled the rest of the album with their favorite black American pop songs. The result was an energetic album
that conveyed a sense of fun and excitement to listeners.

John and Paul continued to write original songs at an extraordinary
pace, and since these were now being performed publicly and recorded,
they knew they needed to secure the publishing rights and royalties for
their music. George Martin introduced the boys to Dick James, who
had a music publishing firm. James set up a company, Northern Songs,
Ltd., with the sole purpose of dealing with Lennon-McCartney tunes.
The income from copyrights on the music would be split 50 percent to
Dick James, 20 percent to Paul, 20 percent to John, and 10 percent to
Brian.[57] Paul later explained that the two wrote music together because
they enjoyed it and they liked to anticipate what the audience could
dance with and enjoy.[58] Paul was not particularly happy that the songs
were consistently credited as "Lennon-McCartney," but John prevailed
in this arrangement. They purposely decided not to include George in
the songwriting credits.

With the success of the single "Please Please Me" and their performance schedule, the Beatles seemed to be everywhere in Britain. They
performed on live radio shows like *Saturday Club* and *Easy Beat,* and
their images and story began to appear regularly in pop magazines like
Boyfriend, which was written for teenaged audiences. The boys also
appeared on regional television shows like *People and Places,* which
aired in the northern part of England.[59] The Beatles had a distinct appearance, with their identical mop-top haircuts and pale-colored suits
with Cardin-style round collars. Some felt they looked more like old-
fashioned women than young men, but young people around Britain
were beginning to copy their style.[60] When they appeared on televi-

sion, Paul played to the camera with his puppy-dog eyes and his unusual Hofner bass. John appeared somewhat defiant, much like he did in his earlier days on stage with the Quarrymen. He stood somewhat stiffly with his feet planted shoulder-width apart and his knees slightly bent. His head was tilted back a bit as he stared down the microphone with squinting eyes. John's formerly white Rickenbacker 325, which he bought in Germany, was now painted black and had a new bridge.

JULIAN

On April 8, 1963, Cynthia gave birth to a baby boy at Sefton General Hospital. John, who was on tour at the time, arrived at the hospital three days later. He had tears in his eyes when he met his son, and as he held the baby for the first time, John examined his son's hands and fingers, asking, "Who's going to be a famous little rocker like his dad, then?"[61] John arranged for Cynthia to have a private room at the hospital. They decided the baby should have a name that reflected their family, so the boy was named John after his father, Charles after Cynthia's father, and Julian after John's mother Julia. But little John Charles Julian Lennon would always be called Julian.

In spite of the excitement of welcoming a new baby to their family, John's relationship with Cynthia was far from idyllic. Much like their art school days, John was often volatile and short-tempered at home. Once when a hairdresser cut Cynthia's hair a bit too short, John yelled at Cynthia and would not speak to her for two days. Cynthia understood that he was under a great deal of pressure and was frequently tired from touring, recording, and writing music, and she tolerated his outbursts and anger. Cynthia wished to provide a stable home for John.

John continued to tour after Julian's birth. The Beatles next single, "From Me to You," was released April 11 and hit the top of the charts within two weeks of its release. John maintained a difficult schedule and when it was finally time for the band to take a short break, he informed Cynthia that he was going on a holiday with Brian Epstein to Barcelona, Spain. Julian was only three weeks old, and of course Cynthia was disappointed, but she tried to understand that John had been working hard and needed a break. No matter what she thought, John was not going to change his plans because of a baby.[62]

While in Spain, Epstein, who was forced to hide his homosexuality while in England because it was illegal, openly introduced John to the gay world. The two attended parties together, and John questioned Brian about which men he found attractive. There were rumors that Brian was in love with John, and John later admitted a one-night stand with Brian to biographer Hunter Davies, but Davies did not believe him. Cynthia also denies this could be possible. Yet some do believe that the two had an affair while in Barcelona, and that their relationship continued until Brian's death.[63]

Others speculated there were power struggles to be sorted out between Brian and John while they were in Spain. Bill Harry of *Mersey Beat* knew them both well and believed Brian wanted to convince John to give Paul more prominence with the Beatles so that the band's successes could grow. Paul, however, thought that John wanted to remind Brian who was in charge.[64] Biographer John Robertson pointed to yet another reason for the two to spend time away from the band: Epstein wanted to convince John that Lennon-McCartney needed to write songs for other, lesser-known artists that Epstein was hoping to launch. John and Paul agreed to this, creating original music for artists like Billy J. Kramer, Peter and Gordon, Mike Shannon, and Cilla Black.[65]

After returning from Spain, John attended Paul's 21st birthday party. While at the party, he beat Cavern announcer Bob Wooler nearly to death with a shovel when Bob insinuated that John was gay. John was also abusive toward Cynthia and another woman at the party. After he realized what he had done to Wooler, John's only concern was the impact his actions might have on his career if Wooler made the story public. Brian sent a telegram to Bob in John's name with an apology and £200 to avert a lawsuit. The *Daily Mirror* carried a short article by journalist Dan Short, who minimized what could have been a disastrous impact by expressing John's remorse and an admission that he was so drunk he did not know what he was doing. The apology was not something John was eager to print, but he knew it was necessary. Soon thereafter, Short because part of the Beatles' press entourage.

Mersey Sound or Liverpop was taking over England. The Scouse accent that defined social class among Liverpudlians was suddenly now chic and accepted. John adopted the accent his Aunt Mimi had raised him to avoid. The public did not mind: The Beatles seemed to be everywhere and their popularity was only growing. They began a weekly radio show called *Pop Go the Beatles* that aired live at 5 PM on Tuesdays. John engaged in humorous verbal exchanges with the announcer between songs. The Beatles fan club was thriving. "She Loves You" was released in July and was instantly a number one hit, the Beatles' third consecutive chart topper. They knew they were on the verge of something big, but none could have anticipated just how big they were going to be.

NOTES

1. Albert Goldman, *The Lives of John Lennon* (New York: William Morrow and Company, 1988), p. 95.

2. Elizabeth Partridge, *John Lennon: All I Want Is the Truth* (New York: Viking Press, 2005), p. 65.

3. Hunter Davies, *The Beatles* (New York: McGraw Hill Publishing, 1985), p. 66

4. Goldman, pp. 97–98.

5. Philip Norman, *John Lennon: The Life* (New York: Harper Collins Publishers, 2008), p. 182.

6. Davies, p. 18.

7. Partridge, p. 68.

8. Ibid., p. 69.

9. Norman, p. 199.

10. Partridge, p. 69.

11. Cynthia Lennon, *John* (New York: Crown Publishers, 2005), p. 57.

12. Partridge, p. 69.

13. Davies, p. 81.

14. Ibid., p. 83.

15. Lennon, p. 58.

16. Ibid., p. 59.

17. Ibid., p. 60.

18. Ibid.

19. Ibid., p. 61.

20. Norman, p. 158.

21. Ibid., p. 205.

22. Davies, p. 100.

23. Partridge, p. 80.

24. Davies, p. 100.

25. Norman, p. 232.

26. Lennon, p. 65.

27. Ibid., p. 70.

28. Davies, p. 105.

29. Robertson, John, *The Art and Music of John Lennon* (New York: Carol Publishing Group, 1991), pp. 7–8.

30. Norman, p. 242.

31. Ibid., p. 243.

32. Ibid., p. 245.

33. Ibid., p. 243.

34. Lennon, p. 80.

35. Norman, p. 264.

36. Ibid., p. 263.

37. Ibid., p. 264.

38. Ibid., p. 265.

39. Ibid., p. 269.

40. Partridge, p. 84.

41. Norman, p. 266.

42. Lennon, p. 89.

43. Norman, p. 271.

44. Lennon, p. 90.

45. Davies, p. 151.

46. Ibid., p. 138.

47. Norman, p. 277.

48. Lennon, p. 91.

49. Norman, p. 276.

50. Lennon, p. 98.

51. Goldman, p. 131.

52. Norman, p. 302.

53. Ibid., p. 287.

54. Ibid., p. 292.

55. Davies, p. 175.

56. Norman, p. 295.

57. Ibid., p. 296.

58. Ibid.

59. Davies, p. 164.

60. Norman, p. 288.
61. Lennon, p. 113.
62. Norman, p. 307.
63. Goldman, pp. 139–40.
64. Norman, p. 307.
65. Robertson, p. 20.

Chapter 4

BEATLEMANIA

In September, the Beatles played the Royal Albert Hall in London, and in October they had top bill on "Val Parnell's Sunday Night at the Palladium" show. Fans lined up all day on Argyll Street outside the Palladium for a glimpse of the boys, a phenomenon that was unprecedented at that time. Hundreds of extra policemen were called in to deal with the crowd, and some later estimated that as many as 2,000 girls mobbed the band as they tried to enter the theater. Hysterical fans screamed, cried, and sometimes fainted when the Beatles were near. Upwards of 15 million people watched the show on television.

All major British newspapers headlined the story the next day, and the term "Beatlemania" was coined to describe the frenzy and hysteria that fans exhibited over the Beatles. Initially slow at catching onto the Beatles phenomenon, the British press, including the *Times*, the *Telegraph* and the various tabloids, soon began printing their pictures and stories at every opportunity. The boys' reputation as fun-loving, affable British lads spread everywhere, and people of all ages and backgrounds were caught up in the excitement. Biographer Hunter Davies, who experienced Beatlemania firsthand, explained the phenomenon as an exaggeration, and he noted how the scenes of mass emotion were difficult to describe in writing because it seemed much more like fiction than reality.

The boys were not the only ones subject to the fans' enthusiasm. Family members experienced the frenzy as well. Beatles fans began calling anyone in Liverpool named McCartney, Lennon, Harrison, or Starkey, hoping to talk to one of the boys or their next of kin. Fans showed up at the Beatles' childhood homes, asking for some artifact from one of the boy's lives, including old socks or a button from their clothes. Some damaged the homes, chipping away at the stones or bricks, or painting "we love you" on the doors and windows.[1] In time, the McCartneys, Harrisons, Starkeys, and Aunt Mimi all needed to move to different homes and towns to escape the excessive interest of fans. Only George's mother seemed to really enjoy the attention.[2]

The Beatles realized that Beatlemania was not just a British phenomenon when they toured Sweden for five days in October 1963. There they were greeted with the same raw emotions fans in England displayed. However, the full extent of Beatlemania did not begin to sink in until the boys arrived at the airport in London after their Swedish tour.[3] Thousands of screaming fans clogged the airport, causing delays for everyone including the prime minister, whose driver was trying to work his way through the traffic. The hysteria caught the attention of an American television host named Ed Sullivan, who was traveling through the airport when the boys arrived.

On November 4, the boys played the Royal Variety Show at the Prince of Wales' Theatre. People considered this to be the biggest show of the year, even bigger than the Palladium.[4] The Beatles began their set with the song "With Love, from Me to You," followed by Paul's solo number "Till There Was You." The live audience included the Queen Mother, Princess Margaret, and Lord Snowdon, and the show aired a week later to an audience of 26 million television viewers. John knew he needed to do something to distinguish himself and the band from the other performers he despised, and perhaps he was aware of critics' comments that the Beatles were beginning to sell out by playing for the establishment rather than rejecting the norms and values of the wealthy.[5] As he faced the crowd before beginning the last song of the performance, John politely asked for the audience's help: "Will the people in the cheaper seats clap your hands, and the rest of you, if you'll just rattle your jewelry." John smiled slightly and bowed away from the microphone, giving a sly thumbs up, and the queen smiled and waved politely from her box as the audience laughed. They closed with "Twist and Shout."

FAMILY LIFE

Given the increased attention from the press, reporters soon discovered Cynthia and Julian, but it no longer mattered. The fact that John was married did not deter Beatles fans, and John finally confessed the truth of his young family to the British public in a biographical piece published in *Mirabelle* magazine in October. John told his story, playing to what he thought the audience would want to hear:

> I think by the way Paul's eyes kept flashing he too liked the German girls but me, I had different ideas. My girl was at home in Liverpool . . . a little while later we were married. I love her. As I'm away such a lot, she lives with Aunt Mimi. I'd like to tell you more about her but I've this old-fashioned idea that marriage is a private thing, too precious to be discussed publicly. So forgive me and understand.[6]

Now that there was no need to hide his family, and since John spent most of his time in London when not touring, the couple found a place to live in the city. The flat was at the top of six flights of stairs, no small matter for Cynthia when she had Julian in his baby carriage and shopping bags to carry, but she was happy to be in London. The location was ideal—near popular clubs, restaurants, and shopping. Even when John was away, there was always something Cynthia could find to do in the city.

John and Cynthia lived near the photographer Bob Freeman, who shot photos of the Beatles for their album covers, and his wife, Sonny, and the couples went out nearly every evening together. Cynthia needed to turn in shortly after they returned home because she rose early to care for Julian, but John preferred to stay up through the wee hours of the morning. He often remained awake until dawn talking with Sonny about books, movies, philosophy, and life in general. Unbeknownst to

Bob or Cynthia, the two had a brief romantic affair, and John later wrote a song about this relationship called "Norwegian Wood."[7]

It did not take Beatles fans long to discover John's new address, and they flocked around his flat at all hours of the day and night. Some were even able to slip inside the building, making their way to the young family's door. Some put chewing gum in the lock to delay John's ability to enter the flat, giving them extra time to see him in person.[8] John tried to be generous with the fans, and if he came home to find a small group gathered outside he signed autographs for them. John understood that it was because of the fans that the Beatles albums sold so well and the concert ticket sales were so high, and he tried to accommodate them as best he could. Unfortunately it was increasingly difficult for the Beatles to move from one location to another because of the screaming and hysterical fans. The newspapers covered their every move, interests, and habits, and Brian Epstein, who was initially pleased for the boys to be getting so much attention, began to worry that they were being overexposed and the public would soon tire of them.[9]

The Beatles second album, *With the Beatles,* was released November 22, 1963. It had 250,000 advance orders, breaking Elvis's *Blue Hawaii* album record of 200,000 advance orders.[10] The album went on to sell more than half a million copies, coming in at the top of the album chart, where *Please Please Me* remained at number two. The single "I Want to Hold Your Hand" went directly to number one. William Mann, classical music critic for the *Times,* named John and Paul the outstanding English composers of 1963.[11] Members of the press clamored to secure interviews with the boys, yet they often asked questions the Beatles found irritating, like "are those wigs you are wearing?" The boys replied with quick, sharp wit.

GOING TO AMERICA

The Beatles went to New York City in February of 1964. Brian Epstein did an incredible amount of work to get them to the United States. The Beatles' album and singles had not done particularly well in the United States to this point, so he had to convince promoters that concert tickets would sell. Sidney Bernstein, an agent with the General Artists Corporation who specialized in teenage music, understood the

phenomenon the Beatles were in Europe and finally encouraged them
to come. He read all about the boys in the British papers and thought
they would be a huge success with American teens. In fact, on a short
tour in France just before leaving for the United States, they learned
that "I Want to Hold Your Hand" had reached number one in the
American charts. It was a big moment for the boys.

Capitol Records, a subsidiary of EMI, posted five million posters an-
nouncing the Beatle's imminent arrival all across the United States.
Fans went wild with anticipation. London's Heathrow Airport was full
of screaming fans when the boys left England, but this paled in com-
parison to the reception the boys received when they landed at New
York's Kennedy Airport. Three thousand screaming fans seemed to be
everywhere, yelling from balconies, clinging to cars, and trying to enter
the room where the press conference was planned.

Upon arrival, the boys were shuffled into a lounge for a press conference. Here they exchanged in quick repartee with reporters:

*The Beatles meet reporters at Kennedy Airport in New York City, February 7,
1964, on their arrival from London for their first American tour. The band
members, from left, are, Paul McCartney, Ringo Starr, George Harrison, and
John Lennon. (AP Photo.)*

Reporter 1:   Will you sing something for us now?
John: We need cash first.
Reporter 2:   When do you rehearse?
John: We don't.
Paul: Yeah, of course we do.
John: Paul does, we don't.
Reporter 3:   But surely you don't need all this police protection?
              Surely you can handle it all yourselves?
John: Maybe you can, you're a lot fatter than we are.[12]

Some would later say this was where the sound bite was invented.

The Beatles stayed at the Plaza Hotel in New York City. Cynthia accompanied John on the trip and was able to experience the hysterical Beatlemania firsthand. Telegraphs, including one from Elvis, gifts, and letters arrived at the hotel in a constant stream. Fans surrounded the hotel, and the boys were confined to their rooms with guards posted at the doors. At one point, Cynthia went to the hotel lobby and was not allowed back into the suite because the officers did not recognize her and they did not believe she was John's wife. Some fans managed to get all the way to the Beatles' suite in spite of the police security, and they assumed she was just another fan.

While in the United States, the Beatles recorded *The Ed Sullivan Show*, playing their hit songs for the live studio audience. Only 700 tickets were available for the studio, but 50,000 fans applied for them. More than 73 million people tuned in on their televisions. It was the most watched television show in the United States up to that point in time. The Beatles also gave their first American concerts. Eight thousand fans attended the show at the Washington Coliseum, and more than 6,000 fans attended two concerts at Carnegie Hall. Many more unsuccessfully sought tickets, including actress Shirley MacLaine, and 300 police officers were called in to provide security for the event.[13] No one could hear their music over the screaming fans, but that did not sway the enthusiasm of the crowds. The boys learned to employ different strategies to enter and exit events, something they turned into a game.

The Beatles had no idea when they left England whether they would be popular in the United States. But Americans embraced them and

The Beatles perform at The Ed Sullivan Show *in New York, February 9, 1964. It was the band's first American appearance and influenced other musicians' future careers. Front row, from left: Paul McCartney, George Harrison, and John Lennon. Drummer Ringo Starr is at rear. (AP Photo.)*

the trip was a huge success. Americans seemed to be looking for some fun and lightness in the gloom that had settled on the nation after President Kennedy's death. The Fab Four, as the boys were sometimes called, seemed to provide the public in general with the diversion they needed, even though the boys were obviously most popular with pre-teen girls.

At the end of two weeks, the Beatles completed their recordings of *The Ed Sullivan Show* and their live concert commitments, and they seemed genuinely glad to return home to London. It was difficult being constantly surrounded by screaming fans, hauled from one place to the next by police officers and tight security. John began to become disillusioned and angry about the fans who claimed to love his music yet threw Jelly Babies at the boys and screamed incessantly through the show, rendering the music inaudible.[14] John also became weary of being polite to the dignitaries who attended the Beatles' shows. He found the experience of being a Beatle more and more horrible and humiliating as their fame grew.[15] The boys became increasingly dependent on one another—they were the only ones who could understand what was happening and the craziness that surrounded them. There was tremendous pressure on them to constantly perform for audiences on live radio, television, and concert venues, to create new music for themselves and others, and they only seemed to add to these demands when they agreed to star in a feature-length film.

A HARD DAY'S NIGHT

Directly after returning home from their first U.S. tour, the Beatles began filming their first movie, A *Hard Day's Night*. United Artists signed the Beatles in advance of their trip, never imagining the group would take America by storm. Instead, United Artists officials thought the Beatles were a flash-in-the-pan pop group, and they offered the boys a one-movie deal and an incredibly small budget that would only allow for a cheap black-and-white film production.[16]

The movie A *Hard Day's Night* played to the pop image of the Beatles, casting the boys in caricatures of their public image. John was not necessarily happy about this, but he went along with the plans for the film anyway. The movie did capture the manic pace of the boys' lives while on tour, and it purposely conveyed an image of the Beatles as decent working-class boys, depicting them as innocent and lovable children.

In spite of the lightness of the movie, the sound track from A *Hard Day's Night* won respect from serious music listeners. The music began to break through the "Mod Mopper" image from their earlier hits,[17] and the Beatles began to experiment with different genres and modes. The title song "A Hard Day's Night" is written in mixolydian mode, an ancient vocal scale that had never been used before in a rock song. Both skiffle and rockabilly's influence are evident in the twangy western style of the music in the movie, particularly in the song "I'll Cry Instead." Rockabilly was an early form of rock music that drew from country and traditional American music as well as from rhythm and blues. Early rockabilly artists included Carl Perkins, Bill Haley, Elvis Presley, and Johnny Cash. Both George Harrison and John Lennon listened to rockabilly music, adopting some of the rhythm patterns and chord changes into Beatles tunes.

John and Paul wrote music continuously, and the year 1964 would turn out to be John's most prolific songwriting period.[18] The two wrote anywhere: in dressing rooms, as they traveled, in hotels, in the studio. One of their favorite places to write was in the basement music room at Paul's girlfriend, Jane Asher's, home.[19] The first 100 Lennon-McCartney songs dealt primarily with puppy love,[20] but as the Beatles' popularity grew, John began to move away from the romantic, optimistic themes that characterized Paul's writing. Instead, John gravitated toward sadder, more blues-style music that was often autobiographical in nature.

Both Paul and John resisted pressure to write in a formulaic way. Rather than create music that sounded more or less the same, they found ways to explore and develop new and different sounds. In part, advances in technology provided previously unexplored creative outlets for them. Beginning late in 1963, for example, double-track recording was possible. Since John was not crazy about the sound of his voice, he began to insist on recording parallel vocal tracks, which allowed him to create different sounds with his voice.

In spite of the Beatles' successes, John yearned to be taken seriously for his intelligence and creative work. He wished to change his image from that of an affable fun-loving Beatle to someone who had an intellectual life and serious creative pursuits. The public's perception was that the Beatles were quite similar, but John knew he was different. He began to set himself apart from the others when his first book was published.

IN HIS OWN WRITE

John's first book, *In His Own Write*, was published three weeks after the Beatles began to work on *A Hard Day's Night*. The book is a collection of short stories, poems, and drawings, evidence of John's imagination and creativity and the influences of *The Goon Show*, Lewis Carroll, and Edward Lear. The book shows Lennon's early preoccupation with violent death and his discomfort with people who had physical handicaps and special needs, but mostly it reflects on Lennon's adolescent interests and humor.

The book had rave reviews and was immediately a best seller in Britain and the United States. The first printing of 100,000 copies sold in the first day.[21] The *Times Literary Supplement* noted that the book was "worth the attention of anyone who fears for the impoverishment of the English language and the British imagination."[22] The public seemed to be pleased to know there was a pop star who could write, although the House of Parliament members questioned how the British educational system could allow for someone to have such "scant regard for standard English usage."[23]

Because of all the attention the book was receiving, John was invited to a Foyle's literary luncheon at the Dorchester Hotel in London, a prestigious event to honor his writing. Seemingly unaware of what a big deal the luncheon would be, John and Cynthia went out to their favorite clubs the night before the event. They showed up at the luncheon with massive hangovers only to find the media and hundreds of people gathered to provide accolades for John's work. John did not expect to give a speech, and he may have been aware of the fact that Brian contacted the hotel the night before to confirm with the event organizers that John would not speak. Apparently the message never reached its intended recipient because the crowd was expecting John to offer a speech. After he was introduced to the audience, John uttered only eight words: "Thank you very much, it's been a pleasure."[24] The audience was disappointed, and some booed, writing it off as a typical Lennon snub to the establishment.

Sales of John's book continued at a high rate, and John began to work on his second book, *A Spaniard in the Works*, which was published a year later. The book was full of cynicism, satire, and wry humor, but it was less autobiographical than John's first book and it did not enjoy the same number of sales. John became known as the intellectual Beatle. He wished to create an image of himself as someone who was interested in something other than screaming girls and guitars.[25]

Shortly after the event at the Dorchester Hotel, John and Cynthia went on a vacation to Ireland with George and his new girlfriend, Patti Boyd, a model he met on the set of *A Hard Day's Night*. When the press discovered this, they camped outside the Dromoland Castle Hotel, where the couples were staying, forcing the young people to plan an escape from the hotel. In a scene reminiscent of their recent film, John and George went out the front door, and Cynthia and Patti were hidden in laundry baskets that were taken from the hotel and placed in the back of a van. Unfortunately, the driver did not realize the girls were in the baskets, and he took them on a harrowing drive to the airport. Soon after, the two couples decided to go to Tahiti where it was less likely screaming fans would accost them. Here they finally had some time to rest, something that was much-needed because they were about to embark on their first ever world tour.

WORLD TOUR 1964

In the summer of 1964, the Beatles took off on a world tour with their first stop in Australia. Biographer Les Norman described it as the first rock tour as we currently understand it, and he wrote that the tour was unique because of its excesses and innocence. As they boys toured, the single "Can't Buy Me Love" broke a worldwide sales record with three million advance copies. It went straight to number one in both England and the United States.

When the Beatles returned to the United States, their road tour included 32 shows in 24 cities in 33 days. The pace was frantic and chaotic as fans swarmed hotels and airports. There were raucous parties in the hotel rooms every night. Derek Taylor, the trusted reporter from Liverpool, was the public relations man, and four correspondents traveled with them, but none betrayed the excesses and indulgences the boys and their crew engaged in. John later recalled:

> Those things are left out, about what bastards we were . . . You have to be a bastard to make it man. That's a fact, and the Beatles were the biggest bastards on earth . . . We were the Caesar. Who was going to knock us when there's a million pounds to be made, all the handouts, the bribery, the police, and the f***ing hype, you know?[26]

People tried to capitalize on the Beatles' popularity everywhere they went. When they checked out of hotel rooms, the beds were stripped, and cut-up sheets were sold to earnest fans. New York supermarkets sold canned "Beatles breath."[27]

As they worked their way across the United States, Kansas business-man Charles O. Finley offered the Beatles $100,000, an unheard-of sum at the time, to perform a concert in Kansas City. When Brian declined, Finley upped the offer to $150,000. When the Beatles agreed to do the show, Finley requested an extra five minutes of performance, offering an additional $50,000 for their time. The Beatles declined, angering Finley, but they went on with the performance, surprisingly to a less-than-sold out audience.

The Beatles concerts received bombs threats in Dallas and Las Vegas, something unheard of for a pop-rock group in those days. Some people believed these were because John refused to do concerts in the Deep South, where audiences were segregated and African Americans could only sit in the back of the venue. John reportedly stated, "We've never played segregated gigs and we're not gonna start now."[28] John seemed to have difficulty understanding the tendency toward violence and racism in the United States.[29]

While in the United States, the Beatles were introduced to other popular musicians. Most notably, they met Bob Dylan, 23 years old and one of the biggest names in American music at the time. Dylan visited with the boys in their New York City hotel. After exchanging initial pleasantries, Brian offered Dylan a drink. When Dylan requested his usual, cheap wine, Brian replied that they only had vintage cham-pagne.[30] But the awkwardness soon dissipated when Dylan rolled a marijuana cigarette in the hotel room, offering the boys their first joint. The effect on John was that he could not stop laughing. After that, whenever he wanted to smoke pot again, he would say, "Let's have a laugh."[31]

Although John was not immediately a fan of Dylan's music, he be-came enthralled with it after George shared *The Freewheelin' Bob Dylan* with him. John and Dylan had a lot in common, and John soon re-alized that Dylan did whatever he wanted, something John admired. John's friendship with Dylan caused him to rethink his approach to songwriting, and he began to incorporate more storytelling into his songs.[32] John wrote "You've Got to Hide Your Love Away" as mimicry of Dylan. The two began a lifelong friendship that resulted in mutual influences on their writing.

In spite of the public smiles and laughter, the weight problems John suffered during this time were indicative of his unhappiness, as were his autobiographical songs "I'm a Loser," "Help," and "Nowhere Man." John was increasingly disillusioned by Beatlemania and the fact that few seemed to care what they sang. Even when the band used 100-watt Vox speakers, the audiences could not hear their music. John did not think people were really interested in his songs so much as they were the public persona of the Beatles. This was quite difficult for him.

On July 6, A *Hard Day's Night* premiered in London with Princess Margaret in attendance. Screaming fans lined the streets at each event, genuinely surprising John.[33] John and Cynthia met Princess Margaret when the film was over. Four days later, the film premiered in Liverpool. John hired a chauffeur to pick up his sisters Jacqui and Julia and Aunt Harrie. Mimi did not attend because she was still visiting relatives in New Zealand. Again, the streets were lined with cheering fans. Before the premiere, the mayor greeted the boys at the town hall, and they waved to the crowds from the balcony. When they arrived at the Odeon theater, they took the stage, again in front of screaming fans. John yelled above the crowd, "Where's me family?"[34] The audience responded with laughter as Jacqui, Julia, and Harrie waved and shouted in return.

KENWOOD

By now, John was earning a considerable amount of money, and he decided to buy a house in Weybridge, Surrey, just outside of London, in part to escape the press of fans on their small flat. In London, fans were always camped outside the building, and Cynthia felt vulnerable when John was away. The couple settled on Kenwood, a large three-story Tudor home situated on one-and-a-half acres of land in St. George's Hill estate. The house was private, and their neighbors were primarily wealthy stockbrokers. Now Cynthia and young Julian would be away from the city and the fans.

When the Lennons moved into their new home in July, they embarked on a massive remodeling project. They hired Ken Partridge, a decorator Brian Epstein recommended. They purchased the house for £20,000, and spent £40,000 on the renovations. While the house was being completely refurbished and a swimming pool was installed outside, the young family stayed in the attic. John insisted they must have cats in their new home, and he named the first one Mimi in honor of his aunt.

It took nine months to complete the renovations, and when Partridge was finished, John and Cynthia changed most of the work he completed. They did not care much for his style, and Partridge had not done everything they hoped. John was especially disappointed because he wanted a mirror installed in the bottom of the swimming pool, but it was not done. The house was quite unique for its time. There was a purple dining room, a state-of-the art kitchen, and a special room for John's books where all the *William* books from his childhood were neatly shelved alongside volumes by Swift, Tennyson, Huxley, Orwell, Tolstoy, and Wilde.[35] John's eclectic possessions were distributed throughout the house, including a gorilla suit he wanted to wear while driving around in his Ferrari.[36]

Even though the house was massive, the Lennons spent most of their family time in a small den at the back of the house. If John was home, he stretched out on a small sofa, reading or daydreaming, or he sat writing a song at the piano with the television playing softly in the background. John was often quiet and reclusive when he was at home, not speaking much to Cynthia or others around him.[37] He liked to have the television on, even if he was not watching it closely.

George and Patti bought a house a few minutes away in Esher, and Ringo and Maureen, who were now married and expecting their first child together, found a place called Sunny Heights on the same estate as John and Cynthia. Paul stayed in London, living in a garret room at the Asher home on Wimpole Street so he could be near his girlfriend, Jane Asher. Jane's father was a psychiatrist and her mother was a woodwind teacher, and they were quite immersed in the cultural and arts scene in London. The Ashers influenced Paul a great deal, and through them he learned much about classic and avant-garde music, which Lennon biographer Albert Goldman credits for moving the Beatles into the art rock scene.[38]

The Beatles became like a second family to one another.[39] They spent their leisure time together, frequently visiting one another's homes. They turned to each other because no one else truly understood what their experiences had been over the past few years. Cynthia later observed that John seemed to relax most in Ringo's company, and he treated George as though he were a younger brother, but she thought he was closest to Paul, even though their relationship was quite complex.[40] John did not spend as much of his free time with Paul.

The *Beatles for Sale* album was released in the fall. The Beatles were no longer smiling from the cover; instead, they struck a more somber pose, staring straight ahead at the camera. John was particularly proud of the intentional feedback sound at the beginning of the album, which he claimed was the first deliberate attempt at distortion in rock music.[41] Roberston describes this album as "the pinnacle of British beat" as well as the "exhaustion of a formula."[42] The Beatles were clearly moving from their pop-rock days into new territory, and the public was poised to hear what was next.

NOTES

1. Hunter Davies, *The Beatles* (New York: McGraw Hill Publishing, 1985).

2. Ibid.

3. Ibid., p. 182.

4. Ibid., p. 181.

5. Elizabeth Partridge, *John Lennon: All I Want Is the Truth* (New York: Viking Press, 2005), p. 93.

6. Philip Norman, *John Lennon: The Life* (New York: Harper Collins Publishers, 2008), pp. 323–24.

7. Sonny's apartment was decorated with Norwegian pine, a cheap wood fashionable at the time.

8. Partridge, p. 94.

9. Davies, p. 187.

10. Ibid., p. 185.

11. Norman, p. 320.

12. Phil Strongman and Alan Parker, *John Lennon and the FBI Files* (London, England: Sanctuary Publishing, 2003), pp. 76–77.

13. Davies, p. 198.

14. Norman, p. 329.

15. Ibid., p. 330.

16. John Robertson, *The Art and Music of John Lennon* (New York: Carol Publishing Group, 1991), p. 30.

17. Goldman, p. 168.

18. Robertson, p. 25.

19. Partridge, p. 98.

20. Goldman, p. 169.

21. Partridge, p. 103.

22. Davies, p. 200.

23. Robertson, p. 27.

24. Cynthia Lennon, *John* (New York: Crown Publishers, 2005), p. 142.

25. Norman, p. 335.

26. Jann Wenner, *Lennon Remembers* (San Francisco, CA: Straight Arrow Books, 2000), p. 64.

27. Norman, p. 369.

28. Strongman and Parker, p. 78.

29. Norman, p. 372.

30. Ibid., p. 375.

31. Ibid., p. 376.

32. Ibid., p. 374.

33. Lennon, p. 146.

34. Ibid.

35. Elizabeth Thomson and David Gutman, *The Lennon Companion: Twenty-Five Years of Comment* (New York: Schirmer Books, 1987), p. 73.

36. Ibid.

37. Davies, p. 346.

38. Goldman, p. 191.

39. Lennon, p. 154.

40. Ibid.

41. Robertson, p. 35.

42. Robertson, p. 34.

Chapter 5

FAME, FORTUNE, AND FANTASY

In 1964, Brian Epstein had made the unlikely prediction that the Beatles would one day be bigger than Elvis, and by 1965, this prediction had, surprisingly, come true. Their music was wildly popular, their faces were among the most recognized in the world, and they were adored everywhere. When the Beatles were just starting out, John often promised the others they were going to the "toppermost of the poppermost!"[1] Little did they know how right he would be, and little could they have predicted how increasingly complicated their lives would become.

One result of the Beatles' worldwide fame was that the boys started to earn some serious money. Although Brian handled the finances for the Beatles, giving each of the boys spending accounts, they soon realized they were growing increasingly wealthy. John and Cynthia found they enjoyed shopping, going out on the town, and participating in one of John's favorite pastimes, buying cars. While the couple was living at Kenwood, John bought a black Rolls Royce with black wheels and black windows. He hired a chauffeur to drive them around to their various commitments, and as his car passed, people wondered if it was the queen or the Beatles.[2] The Rolls was equipped with a television, a folding bed, a writing desk, a refrigerator, and a telephone, even though John, who was often technologically challenged, experienced difficulty using the telephone.[3] John bought Cynthia a white Austin Mini Cooper, and he also purchased a gold Porsche and a red Ferrari, his favorite to drive. John obtained his driver's license when he was 25 years of age, but he was a terrible driver. He did not like to use the brakes, and he never seemed to learn to maneuver the gearshift, which meant his cars often needed to have repairs.[4]

The couple liked to socialize with their celebrity friends. When John appeared on the television show *Not Only . . . But Also*, he met Peter Cook and Dudley Moore, who starred on the popular BBC series. Cook was a comedian and writer who became known as one of the leading figures of the 1960s satire boom in England, and Moore was an actor, comedian, and musician. John got along well with Peter, and John and Cynthia socialized with Peter, his wife Wendy, and Dudley Moore on several occasions. In addition to the Beatles, other regular guests at the Lennon home included Mike Nesmith of the Monkees, Bob Dylan, and folk singer Joan Baez. Bob and Sonny Freeman visited regularly with their son, yet neither Robert nor Cynthia ever suspected John and Sonny formerly had a romantic relationship.

Although the Lennons moved into the downstairs of the Kenwood house after they altered the renovations to suit their own tastes, John spent a great deal of time in the attic. Here he set up a small recording studio where he wrote songs and listened to music. Lyrics and tunes came to John at any time of the day or night, and he sometimes jumped out of bed after falling asleep to capture something that came to him while sleeping. Paul visited frequently, usually spending about two or three hours at a time with John as they wrote songs together. Their working practices remained very similar to when they wrote at Paul's childhood home years before. John woke up when Paul arrived, and the two chatted while Paul had some tea and cornflakes. Then they would get their guitars and work on music.[5] Sometimes John called Paul when he was working on something new, singing to him or playing a new tune over the telephone.[6] They still didn't record their music at this stage of a song's development; instead, they held to their longstanding belief that if they could remember the song the next day it was a good one. This all began to change in 1965 when they began to write more independently, one developing most of a lyric or melody before sharing it with the other.[7] John often wrote by building songs on sequences of chords while he sat at the piano with the television on. Once he had some chord sequences, he focused on the words of the song, the most important element to him.[8] The melody was the last piece that he finalized. John's process was different than that of Paul, who focused on the melody first and then tried to develop lyrics for the music. Neither had formal music training, something that may have allowed them to be more uninhibited and creative as they worked with unique chords and sounds, although their recording work with George Martin certainly taught them a few more formal things about music.

According to Paul, John was not particularly confident with his songwriting, and when he played something for the first time, John first asked Paul what he thought, and then what they should do with it.[9] John was never satisfied with much, including his own voice, and he always insisted on wearing headphones when they recorded so that the sound of his own voice could be distorted. He remained insecure about his guitar playing.[10] Paul explained that to John, things were always better in his mind than they were in real life.[11] In spite of this, George Martin remembered that John was easier to work with in the studio than Paul was. John allowed the other Beatles to create as they worked on a song; in contrast, Paul knew exactly how he wanted songs to sound, and he often played the guitar and drum parts for George and Ringo so that they could get the song just right.[12] John, on the other hand, was not always particularly practical, and sometimes he did not even tune his guitar.[13]

In the studio, John and Paul were free from the pressures of live performances and screaming fans, and they were able to create whatever they wished. They layered sounds and added tracks to get the various effects they wanted. The studio was one of the few private places they enjoyed, and as early as 1963, Paul declared it their favorite venue.[14] They generally got along well in the studio, and if they disagreed, their arguments were short-lived. Paul and John always challenged one another through their music, pushing for new and different ideas in their work.

Cynthia remembered the times at Kenwood as generally happy. When John was not writing music or reading, he liked to play with

Scalextric car racing. He had three electric tracks set up in the attic at Kenwood to race the miniature cars. John sometimes teamed up with Julian to race Paul, George, or Ringo. When John was on tour, he wrote letters to Cynthia with jokes and stories, often telling her how much he missed her and Julian. In August 1965 while on tour of the United States, he wrote a particularly poignant letter about his love for Julian and his wish to spend more time with him:[15]

> I really miss him as a *person* now—do you know what I mean— he's not so much "the baby" or "my baby" anymore he's a real living part of me now . . . I can't wait to see him, I miss him more than I've ever done before—I think it's been a slow process my feeling like a *real father*.[16]

John certainly knew what it was like to have an absent father, particularly as a young boy, and he undoubtedly recognized the eerily similar parallels between Alf as a father and himself.

It often took John a few days to recover when he returned from a tour, and he often slept quite a bit during his first days home. Once he rested, he tried to catch up on everything he could, including family news and fan mail. John explained the mail to Julian by saying, "Look, Julian . . . these letters are very important. They're our bread and butter. See? This one is your breakfast, that one's your dinner, and this one is a new guitar for Daddy."[17] John could be quite edgy at home, and he sometimes vented his anxiety and pent up anger on Cynthia and Julian. John's moods were often unpredictable, and it was hard to know if he might become impatient with the boy, so Cynthia preferred that John spend time with him in small bursts.

MEMBERS OF THE ORDER OF THE BRITISH EMPIRE

In June 1965, Queen Elizabeth delivered news that would shock the Beatles and much of Britain when she announced that each of the boys would be made Members of the Most Excellent Order of the British Empire (MBEs)[18] at the Queen's Birthday Honours, the celebration of her official birthday. Brian called John to tell him the good news, and John was excited but a bit surprised. He responded to Brian by saying:

> F***in' hell, Brian, you must be f***ing joking. Why? Pop stars don't get MBEs, they're supposed to be for ex-army, do-gooders, the establishment. Bloody hell, wait till I tell Cyn and Mimi.[19]

John's misgivings were not unwarranted. When former recipients of the MBE heard the Beatles would receive this honor, they returned their medals in protest.

The boys went to Buckingham Palace to receive the awards. They found the experience to be quite amusing, breaking into laughter as the officials told them how to curtsey and what to do when they met the queen. Although he joked around with the others while he was there, John later expressed his disillusionment with the experience to biographer Hunter Davies:

> I really think the Queen believes in it all. She must. I don't believe in John Lennon, Beatle, being any different from anyone else, because I know he's not. I'm just a feller. But I'm sure the Queen must think she's different. I always hated all the social things. All the horrible events and presentations we had to go to. All false. You could see right through them all and all the people there. I despised them.[20]

He briefly considered turning down the award, but Brian told him it was impossible. John felt as though he had finally sold out.[21]

Mimi had a different view of the situation. She finally seemed to be proud of John, and so he gave the MBE to her. She displayed it with pride on top of her television set for a number of years. But Mimi also understood the downside to all this fame. She shared with John how the fans were becoming quite a problem for her. She wanted to move from Liverpool to a more private location. John and Cynthia helped Mimi to find a beach home in the port city of Poole, located in Dorset on the south coast of England. Mimi sold Mendips, and John bought her the new home and provided her a weekly allowance. John also bought a house for Cynthia's mother and furnished her with a weekly

Beatle John Lennon smiles as he poses with his Member of the Order of the British Empire medal (MBE), presented to the Beatles by the Queen of England in a ceremony at Buckingham Palace, in London, England on October 26, 1965. (AP Photo.)

allowance. Of course when Mimi found out, she was a bit annoyed that Cynthia's mother's allowance was the same as her own.[22]

John's generosity extended to his sisters, who he treated to shopping trips in London, and to his friends. He gave Pete Shotton, his old school friend, £20,000 to open a supermarket on Hayling Island. The store was located close to where the Lennons were living in Kenwood, and Pete often stopped by to visit his now famous friend. They hung out together in the attic, racing John's elaborate toy cars and sharing stories about their school days when life was certainly much simpler and perhaps more fun.

BACK TO THE UNITED STATES

In August, the Beatles' third American tour began. The tour lasted 17 days. To accommodate the large crowds of fans, the Beatles performed primarily in baseball stadiums across the country. The first and most lucrative was Shea Stadium, where Ed Sullivan introduced them to screaming fans. The boys, dressed in outfits that looked like military uniforms, complete with epaulets, brass buttons, and sheriff's badges, ran across the ball field and onto the center field stage to play for more than 55,000 people. Two thousand security personnel were hired to handle the crowds, including the many young girls who tried to run across the ball field from the stands to the stage.

The Beatles played just 30 minutes amid deafening screams from the crowd. They couldn't hear themselves or one another, even with the large Vox speakers, and when John traded his Rickenbacker guitar for the organ, he began to play with his elbows because he found the event to be so ridiculous. Paul and George cracked up as they watched him. In spite of the fact that no one heard their music, they had some reason to smile—the show grossed $304,000, the highest amount of money for a single concert event in the history of show business up to that date.[23]

From New York they traveled across the country to Atlanta, Chicago, Houston, Portland, and California, facing similar hysteria among the fans. Most shows began with John singing lead on "Twist and Shout," followed by Paul leading on "She's a Woman." Then John picked up lead again on "I Feel Fine" and "Dizzy Miss Lizzy," followed by John and Paul singing "Ticket to Ride," "Baby's in Black," and "A Hard Day's Night." George's solo was on "Everybody's Trying to Be My Baby," and Ringo sang either "Act Naturally" or "I Want to Be Your Man." John often included "Help!" in the lineup, and then typically closed with "I'm Down." The boys played two shows at the Hollywood Bowl in Los Angeles and finished at the Cow Palace in San Francisco.

FAMILY MATTERS

Fame and fortune could not prevent John from experiencing more loss and tragedy in his family. In December, Bobby Dykins was killed in a car crash. John was not told about the accident until much later, and he was quite upset to learn that his sisters were now orphans and he had been unaware of their loss. When John learned that Harrie was named his sisters' guardian, he bought her a house that he wished for the girls to eventually inherit.[24] Julia was 18 years of age, and Jacqui was 16 when their father died, and John knew they still needed a home and someone to look after them. John intended for the house to belong to his sisters, but his accountant advised that he keep it in his name, just as he did all the other houses he bought.[25]

Although John did not spend a great deal of time with his family, he did care about them and wanted them to be comfortable and well cared for. The one exception was his father Alf, who suddenly appeared unannounced at Kenwood. John greeted him in a disinterested way, asking simply what he wanted.[26] Cynthia later wrote that Alf turned up at Kenwood only after someone pointed out to him that John was a millionaire. Their initial reunion was a bit awkward and brief, with Alf assuring John that he only wanted the chance to tell his side of the story.[27] John was initially surprised at the resemblance he bore to his father, but Alf was stunned by the resemblance he saw between John and Julia.[28]

Alf was savvy enough to realize he could benefit financially from his connection to John. He sold his story to a magazine, and released a record titled *That's My Life (My Love and My Home)*. John thought it was awful and he was embarrassed by it.[29] With his newfound fame, Alf gained some measure of personal confidence. He began dating a 19-year old young woman named Pauline, whom he later married. He was 56 years old at the time.

PSYCHEDELIC EXPERIENCES

Acid and drug use was becoming more widespread among youth in Britain as traditional social mores were challenged and loosened. Whereas the 1950s had been a time of stability and conformity in England, the 1960s were a time for upheaval and change. The National Health Service began to distribute oral contraceptives that, combined with the feminist movement, contributed to a greater sense of independence among women. John Robinson's book *Honest to God*, published in 1963, captured debates within the Church of England as church attendance declined and religious experiences seemed less important to people. Social unrest due to economic difficulties among trade unions in particular, along with the publication of E. P. Thompson's book *The Making of the English Working Class*, provoked youth to question authority. Young girls began to wear mini skirts, made popular by London designer Mary Quant, and men and women alike began to let their hair grow long as they donned paisley, stripes, and other colorful clothing.

The Beatles were key figures as these changes evolved. They let their hair grow longer, and John sported long sideburns and eventually a beard. They wore paisley patterns and less conventional clothes, and experimented with music and drugs. John and the other Beatles smoked marijuana fairly regularly after Bob Dylan first introduced them to it in New York City, and in the mid-1960s they added LSD (lysergic acid diethylamide) to their experimentation. John's first experience with LSD was when he and Cynthia had coffee that was laced with the drug at a dinner party hosted by dentist John Riley.[30] At the time, LSD was considered to be a way to expand human understandings of the mind and subconscious, something that intrigued John. He was fascinated with the experience and began to use LSD regularly.[31] George and Patti were also at the party and shared the experience with the Lennons, and as a result John's relationship with George changed. The two began to spend more time together, and even though Paul had been George's friend the longest, George believed he became closer to John from this point on.[32]

The same could not be said for the connection between John and Cynthia. John tried to persuade Cynthia to join him in his drug use, but she did not like the experience she had with LSD, nor did she wish to have the false intimacy she thought LSD brought with other people.[33] Soon John was seeking out more LSD, putting acid-laced sugar cubes on his tongue to melt or eating a small blotter paper drenched in the drug.[34] He began to go out in the evenings, seeking company from those who shared his fascination with the effects of the drug, and Cynthia often woke up in the morning to find their home full of people who were stoned and wanting something to eat.[35]

John read about LSD in books like *The Psychedelic Experience* and *The Psychedelic Reader,* written by Timothy Leary, Ralph Metzner, and Richard Alpert. These books were considered to be the Bible of the LSD movement. As his experiences with LSD evolved, John began to write about drug experiences in his music, beginning with the song "To-morrow Never Knows," which included lyrics lifted from Leary's book: "Whenever in doubt, turn off your mind, relax, float downstream."[36]

Around this time, John also began to experiment more with sound, describing the effect he wished to create to sound technician Geoff Emerick. Geoff would use his imagination and the limited technological devices available to him to make what John heard in his mind into sounds that could be recorded, something ever more challenging as John delved deeper into LSD.

HELP!

In July 1965, the Beatles' second film, *Help!*, premiered. It was almost as successful as *A Hard Day's Night*. The movie was a spoof on then-popular action adventure, James Bond-style films. In the movie, members of an Eastern cult want to obtain a ring from Ringo's finger, and they pursue the boys through many misadventures to get the ring. The film was shot in color on site in England, the Bahamas, and the Austrian Alps. John's standout song was "You've Got to Hide Your Love Away," which is evidence of Dylan's influence on him at that time.

An album of the same name, *Help!*, was released a month after the film and included Paul's ballad "Yesterday." Although this film was not as popular as *A Hard Day's Night*, both the album and the movie went to the top of the charts. Mimi went to the premiere, but she did not like the film.[37] John did not disagree. He was not particularly pleased with the experience or the end result either. John later observed that he felt like an extra:

> The movie was out of our control. With *A Hard Day's Night*, we had a lot of input, and it was semi-realistic. But with *Help!*, Dick Lester didn't tell us what it was all about. I realize, looking back, how advanced it was. It was a precursor for the *Batman* "Pow! Wow!" on TV—that kind of stuff. But he never explained it to us. Partly, maybe, because we hadn't spent a lot of time together between *A Hard Day's Night* and *Help!*, and partly because we were smoking marijuana for breakfast during that period. Nobody could communicate with us, it was all glazed eyes and giggling all the time. In our own world. It's like doing nothing most of the time, but still having to rise at 7 AM, so we became bored.[38]

The movie did seem to be an early forerunner of early music videos, and the movie's style was later adapted in a television series for the pop band The Monkees.

RUBBER SOUL

The sixth Beatles studio album, *Rubber Soul*, was released in December 1965, along with the single "Day Tripper," which became the 10th consecutive Beatles record to go directly to the number one spot on the British charts. Lennon's songs on *Rubber Soul* demonstrate his move away from "pop" Beatles or "Beatle John" as he continued to experiment with sound and convention. The Abbey Road studio where the Beatles recorded their albums now had a four-track recording set-up, allowing them to experiment with instrumentals, vocals, and other sounds until they had the recording just right. They were writing songs with complex chords and harmonies, and experimenting with musical forms. John enjoyed reversals of convention and created role-reversed love songs like "(Baby You Can) Drive My Car," which cleverly inverted boy/girl roles.

The song "Norwegian Wood" was a more sophisticated take on the modern woman, an autobiographical piece about his relationship with Sonny Freeman. George played sitar, a stringed instrument with a long hollow neck and gourd chamber that has been played for centuries in India, Pakistan, and Bangladesh. This was George's first recorded solo on the instrument and perhaps more notably the first time a sitar was used on a rock album. George found Indian music to be fascinating, and John caught onto George's enthusiasm. He explained to reporter Maureen Cleave, "This music is thousands of years old; it makes me laugh, the British going over there and telling them what to do. Quite amazing."[39]

Rubber Soul was a critical and commercial success. Marijuana and musical maturation contributed to the more sensuous nature of album. John tried in parts to emulate Dylan, writing autobiographical songs that had more of a narrative and journalistic style like "In My Life" and "Nowhere Man." Through his music, he captured the places and people that were part of his childhood.

The single "Paperback Writer" was released in May 1966 with the song "Rain" on the B-side. This song marked a recording landmark of sorts as the first recorded piece to intentionally use backward tapes. Lennon accidentally discovered the potential of this technique when he was working in his recording studio at home. "Paperback Writer" did not reach number one on the charts.

THE FINAL TOUR

In June 1966, the Beatles embarked on what would be their final tour. They went first to Hamburg, where they reconnected with Astrid Kirchherr and other acquaintances from their earlier days in the city. This would be the only European city on their tour. From Hamburg, they went to Tokyo, the Philippines, and finally the United States. Live video of these performances show fans screaming with emotion when they saw the boys, but such reactions were harmless compared to what happened behind the scenes. In Tokyo, a group of fanatical right-wing students threatened to kill the Beatles for performing at Nippon Budokan, a national shrine to the Japanese war dead where Sumo wrestling and martial arts displays were typically held. Death threats against pop stars were unprecedented at this time, and city officials mobilized approximately 35,000 police and security guards to protect the Beatles during their four days in the city.[40]

When the boys left Tokyo, their troubles were not over. Just a week later, the Beatles were again frightened for their lives in Manila, Philippines. Here, Brian made an error by turning down an invitation for the boys to meet Imelda Marcos, wife of Philippine President Ferdinand Marcos, at an official reception that included 300 children at the Malacañang Palace. This did not leave the Beatles in good favor with the Filipino government or people. The Beatles needed to make a frantic escape from the island, and as their plane was about to depart, Brian had to pay a significant sum of money to get the entourage out of the country.[41]

The *Revolver* album was released in early August as the boys continued to tour. As Peter Clayton of *Gramophone* explained, the album was

> an astonishing collection, and listening to it you realize that the distance these four odd young men have travelled since that first record of "Love Me Do" in 1962 is musically even greater than it is materially. It isn't easy to describe what's here, since much of it

involves things which are either new to pop music or which are being properly applied for the first time.[42]

Some of the more notable songs included "Taxman," "Eleanor Rigby," and "Yellow Submarine," which elicited support from Brian Jones, Marianne Faithfull, and others to create the sound effects. John wanted to capture the sound of singing under water for "Yellow Submarine," and after a few experiments, sound designer Geoff Emerick decided to place a microphone sealed in a condom in a glass water bottle to get the effect they needed.[43] In the song "Tomorrow Never Knows," John told George Martin and Geoff Emerick he wanted to sound like the Dalai Lama shouting from a mountaintop, so they used rotating Leslie speakers from a Hammond organ to get the effect John imagined.[44] Hamburg friend Klaus Voorman provided the cover art for the album. This album, which used automatic double tracking, later became known as one of the greatest albums in rock history.

After events in Japan and the Philippines, the Beatles began to discuss the need to stop touring. Their personal safety was at risk, along with that of their crew, and they were discouraged that fans did not seem to care about the music during their performances. To further complicate matters, just a few months before the tour began, John gave an interview to journalist Maureen Cleave of the *London Evening Standard*. John had known Maureen for years and was comfortable with her. He told Maureen:

> Christianity will go. It will vanish and shrink. I needn't argue with that; I'm right and I will be proved right. We're more popular than Jesus now; I don't know which will go first—rock'n'roll or Christianity. Jesus was all right but his disciples were thick and ordinary. It's them twisting it that ruins it for me.[45]

When the interview was published, no one in England seemed to be concerned, but when it was reprinted in the United States in a magazine called *Databook*, many Americans were infuriated. Radio stations began to ban Beatles music, John received hate mail, and psychics predicted that John would be shot while he was in the United States.[46] Brits at the time interpreted Christianity as being synonymous with

the Church of England, and with church attendance on the decline
in England, few seemed to disagree with John's claim, if they cared
about it at all.[47] Among the more fervently religious Americans, however, there was a backlash against the Beatles. Young people smashed
and burned albums and other Beatles memorabilia on the streets, and
religious leaders across the country damned the boys and anyone who
bought the Beatles' music.

Although the Beatles were concerned about their safety when they
left London on August 11, 1966, John and Paul attempted to put on
a brave face to reporters who questioned whether they were worried
about the reception they would receive in America. Later John admitted that he was scared by the reports of American's reaction to him and
he had initially wanted to cancel the tour. John explained:

> I thought they'd kill me, because they take things so seriously [in
> the United States]. I mean they shoot you and then they realize it
> wasn't that important. So I didn't want to go, but Brian and Paul
> and the other Beatles persuaded me.[48]

In spite of this, the Beatles continued with the tour, stopping first in
Chicago. Once on the ground in the United States, they quickly realized that John would need to offer a statement to the press to help quell
the anger among the American public. John feared he would ruin the
tour unless something was done, and he would rather apologize publicly
than face his bandmates if his statement caused them to fail. At the
Astor Towers Hotel in Chicago, John offered an extended monologue
to the press, rather than reciting from a prepared statement:

> I'm not anti-God, anti-Christ or anti-religion. I was not knocking
> it. I was not saying we were greater or better . . . not comparing
> us with Jesus Christ as a person or God as a thing or whatever . . .
> People think I'm anti-religion, but I'm not. I'm a most religious
> fellow . . . I'm sorry I opened my mouth.[49]

When pressed about whether he was prepared to apologize, Lennon
offered further clarification:

I believe in God but not as an old man in the sky . . . I believe
what people call God is something in all of us.[50]

He ended the press conference by saying:

I'm sorry I said it really, I never meant it to be a lousy anti-religious
thing. I apologize if that will make you happy. I still don't know
quite what I've done. I've tried to tell you what I did do but if you
want me to apologize, if that will make you happy, then okay, I'm
sorry.[51]

The media attending the press conference seemed to forgive John, and
Brian decided they should continue with the tour, including the concerts that had already been scheduled in more religiously conservative
areas of the Deep South. Unfortunately the media did not necessarily
reflect the views of the American public. Enraged people stood outside concert venues with signs that read "Beatles Go Home" and "Jesus
Died for You Too, John Lennon."[52]

Television news aired coverage of protests outside performance venues. Even after John's public apology, young people continued to protest
against the Beatles in the streets, and Ku Klux Klan members paraded
outside the Washington, DC, concert. The boys were under the tight-
est security possible as they remained in guarded hotel rooms. When
the Beatles performed at the Mid-South Coliseum in Memphis, Ten-
nessee, the sound of a gunshot rang out. Everyone looked immediately
at John and then at one another to be sure no one was hurt. It turned
out to be the sound of a firecracker launched by someone perhaps as a
cruel joke, but no one would have been surprised if it had been more
serious. Four days later at the Shea Stadium performance, 11,000 seats
were unsold.[53] John was miserable.

The Beatles' final live performance for a paying audience was at Candlestick Park in San Francisco, California, on August 29, 1966. The
stage was set up over second base in the middle of the baseball field,
far from the fans screaming in the stadium seats. The boys opened with
"Rock and Roll Music." Signs draped in the stadium picked up on the
controversy over John's comments about Christianity. One had a cross

in the middle and read "Lennon Saves" in bold block print. Their final song was "Long Tall Sally."

When the Beatles first went to America, they did not know if they would meet with failure as so many other British acts had before them. When they returned to Britain after their last American concert, they succeeded not only in the fame and fortune they experienced but they also opened the American market for other British acts to follow.[54]

LIFE AFTER TOURING

The boys were tired of touring and performing for audiences that did not really listen to them. John was particularly concerned that the commercialization of the Beatles reduced them to a formula,[55] and he was similarly fed up with all the pretending that went along with being a Beatle.[56] John was indifferent about the Beatles' music and he had become disillusioned by the experience. He referred to himself and the Beatles as a con:

> We're a con as well. We know we're conning them, because we know people want to be conned. They've given us freedom to con them. . . . People think the Beatles know what's going on. We don't. We're just doing it. People want to know what the inner meaning of "Mr. Kite" was. There wasn't any. I just did it. I shoved a lot of words together then shoved some noise on. I just did it. I didn't dig that song when I wrote it. I didn't believe in it when I was doing it.[57]

One consequence of John's disinterest in being a Beatle was that he became more casual in his political statements. The Vietnam War raged on, and although Great Britain did not send troops to South Vietnam and there was no military draft in England at the time, young people throughout England still engaged in protests against the war. Antiwar marches and demonstrations developed into what came to be known as the underground, a movement that included poetry performances, rock music, and LSD. Paul, who was living in London at the time, was the Beatle closest to this action, yet John, an avid newspaper reader, was well aware of these happenings. At a New York press conference, John went against Brian's longstanding advice to avoid commenting on the war. He told the press assembled to meet the Beatles "We think of it every day. We don't like it. We don't agree with it. We think it is wrong."[58] John was well aware of the atrocities of the war, the seemingly futile attempts to end it by protestors, and he long wished to speak out. His international celebrity coupled with his antiwar position did not go unnoticed.[59]

While all four of the boys agreed they should stop touring, they were not sure what to do when it was over, and the transition seemed particularly concerning to John. John decided to take a small part in a film called *How I Won the War*, a movie about a fictional squad of British soldiers in the North African campaign who are given the task of establishing the central part of a cricket field, called the pitch, behind enemy lines. It is a farce intended to expose the lunacy of war and war movies.[60] Actors speak directly to the camera and to one another as they make their way through the comical British plot. John played the role of Private Gripweed, and his costume included round, wire-rim glasses that soon became part of his everyday attire. The director and producer was Richard Lester, who John knew from *Hard Day's Night* and *Help!* The film conveyed a subtle antiwar theme, which some claimed was part of John's attraction to the role, even though England was not engaged in a military conflict at the time.[61] John's role in the film ends with Gripweed mortally wounded by a gunshot,[62] holding his stomach as he looks into the camera and says, "I knew this would happen, you knew this would happen didn't you?"

Film scenes were shot in Germany and Spain. Beatles road manager Neil Aspinall travelled with John for the entire length of the shoot, and John's chauffeur, Les Anthony, arrived on site with John's Rolls Phantom V. John had an extensive record collection in the car, along with external stereo speakers that allowed him to share his music and various sound effects with anyone who happened to be on the street at the time.

When the cast and crew arrived in Almería, Spain, John invited Cynthia and Julian to join him. Ringo and his wife, Maureen, also joined them for a short holiday. While the film had good reviews and Lester was complimentary of John's work, John decided that acting was not his first love. Instead, he wanted to focus on music, and as he

Beatle John Lennon is shown with his hair cut short for his role in How I Won the War *in 1966 at an unknown location. The movie was filmed in Germany. (AP Photo.)*

turned his attention to songwriting, he relied on memories of his childhood in Woolton. Although he was in the Mediterranean a the time, John began to write about the orphanage, called Strawberry Field, located behind his Aunt Mimi's house, transforming it into a dreamy ethereal song.

Taking a slight diversion from his music, John attended an exhibition at John Dunbar's art gallery, the Indica, on November 7, 1966. The exhibition, called a happening,[63] was by Japanese artist Yoko Ono. When John entered the gallery, Yoko handed him a card that read "Breathe." He panted at her. Yoko gave him a tour of the exhibit, offering that he could hammer a nail into an empty canvas and encouraging him to climb a ladder where he used a magnifying lens to read the word "yes" written in tiny script on a card on the ceiling. John found Yoko's work to be humorous and creative.

Soon after meeting John, Yoko sent him a copy of her book *Grapefruit* along with many cards and letters, and she went to Kenwood on several occasions hoping to meet him. Dunbar later stated that "if he had set out to destroy John Lennon, he could not have done better than to introduce him to Yoko Ono."[64] Yoko began to pursue John with intensity, waiting outside Apple studios for him to appear, ultimately capturing John's curiosity and attention because of her strength, aggressiveness, and persistence. Soon John and Yoko were privately courting in the back of the limo as chauffeur Les Anthony drove them around town.[65]

Cynthia knew something was wrong and she felt increasingly insecure. John was never one to communicate well. Sometimes when he was home days would pass before he would say anything,[66] but she sensed that things were changing. The distance between her and John was growing, and Yoko Ono added a strange and uneasy dimension to their relationship. Cynthia had plastic surgery on her nose, believing this would make a difference in her confidence. John tried to discourage her, but let her proceed with the operation. Afterward, no one seemed to notice the change in her appearance.

John Lennon and his wife, Cynthia, in a 1966 photo. (AP Photo.)

In spite of the complexities of his personal life, John continued to write songs with Paul. Even though the Beatles were no longer touring, they needed to produce albums to fulfill their recording contracts. Their primary competition was the Rolling Stones, their long time friends. Other American bands that were big at the time included the Beach Boys, Lovin' Spoonful, Frank Zappa and the Mothers of Invention, and Bob Dylan's new synthesis of folk and rock music in the album *Blonde on Blonde*. Dylan continued to push John musically, as John did Dylan, and when he visited London in 1966 on tour, the two hung out together.

The "Strawberry Fields Forever"/"Penny Lane" single was released in February 1967. The Beatles pushed the boundaries of convention yet again musically, and they continued to challenge the conventions of the record industry by insisting both songs were equally marketable and refusing to put either song on the B-side of the album. Instead Martin issued the disc as a double A-side just as they had done with singles for "Day Tripper"/"We Can Work It Out" and "Yellow Submarine"/"Eleanor Rigby." While the songs both conjured images from Lennon and McCartney's childhood, they couldn't be more different. Whereas "Strawberry Fields Forever" was dense, dreamy, and complicated, "Penny Lane" was clear, upbeat, and cheerful. Penny Lane in Liverpool was part of all the Beatles' childhoods, but it had particular resonance for John: his father went to school on Penny Lane, and years later his mother worked in a café on Penny Lane. John lived near the street as a very young child before he moved to Aunt Mimi's house. And in 1966, John had a tragic connection to the street after Bobby Dykins's fatal car crash into a Penny Lane lamppost.

"Strawberry Fields Forever" was created over a five-week period as the boys experimented with different instruments and sounds during more than 55 hours in the studio.[67] The end result was two different versions of the song, and John could not decide which he liked better. He asked George Martin to splice the two songs together, using the beginning of one recording and the end of another, but the songs were in different keys and tempos. Martin was not daunted, however, and worked to blend the two versions using a frequency changer and other technical skills.

The single did not go directly to the top of the charts like all the other singles the Beatles had released since "Please Please Me." Instead, it remained number two on the British charts, behind Engelbert Humperdinck's song "Release Me." Some critics wondered if the boys, who were no longer touring and seemed intent on creating songs in the studio that would be impossible to replicate for a live audience, were on their way out. But over the next few months the Beatles continued on, and between November 1966 and March 1967, they logged 700 hours in the studio. When they did not have an album together in time for Christmas, Martin assembled a series of previous hits that he titled A Collection of Beatles Oldies . . . but Goldies. Not easily discouraged, the boys worked closely with George Martin to create the music as it unfolded in the studio, using new technologies developed with sound engineer Geoff Emerick to splice songs, sounds, and tempos into masterpieces. John and Paul argued over songs, continuing to compete with one another as they worked, nudging one another to create more provocative lyrics and tunes. Their competition contributed to the quality and creativity of the songs and produced some of their best collaborative efforts.

John's songwriting continued to draw heavily on his everyday experiences. On January 17, 1967, as the Beatles finished recording "Penny Lane," John read the Daily Mail, in which there was a story about several thousand holes in the streets of Blackburn, Lancashire. Two days later, the Beatles began to record his new song that retold this story, "A Day in the Life." Martin brought a 41-piece orchestra into the studio to create the sounds John imagined for the piece. As the orchestra members donned carnival hats and clown faces, Martin instructed them to go from the lowest note to the highest note on their instrument, getting louder as they went into the higher registers. The results linked sections of the song, and the final sustained piano chord added to the interesting elements of the piece. "A Day in the Life" was banned on many British and American radio stations for being too provocative. Listeners assumed that the man who "blew his mind out in a car" was on LSD, that the middle section contained a reference to smoking pot, and that the instrumental section by the orchestra was intended to replicate a drug-induced delirium.

"Lucy in the Sky with Diamonds" came from a drawing John's son Julian brought home from school about his friend Lucy O'Donnell.[68] The song was an adult fairy tale that strung together random phrases like tangerine trees and marmalade skies.[69] The song was banned by the BBC because the first letters of each main word in the title spelled out the letters LSD; however, John denied any connection to the drug. Although Paul supported the story about Julian's drawing, those who knew John and his creative uses of language were doubtful.[70] The song became one of the most popular on the album and set a standard for psychedelic rock among British bands like Pink Floyd.

When visiting an antique shop in Kent, John was drawn to a poster from Pablo Fanque's circus that listed jobs for various members of the circus. The song "Being for the Benefit of Mr. Kite" followed. John told George Martin that he wanted to smell the sawdust on the circus floor when the song was produced. Martin and sound designer Geoff Emerick used tape loops of a musical steam organ that he randomly put together to get the effect John imagined. The song was banned from radio in Britain because the phrase "Henry the Horse" combined two words that independently were slang expressions for heroin.

John's inspiration for the song "Good Morning, Good Morning" came from a Kellogg's Corn Flakes commercial that used this phrase. One day as he sat at the piano writing, the phrase from a corn flakes advertisement caught his attention.[71] The song also had interesting sound innovations as John asked Emerick to arrange animal sounds at the end of the track. He wanted the sound of the animals to occur in order so that the first animal could be devoured by the next. The final clucking chicken sound transforms into a guitar that leads to the next song on the album—"Sgt. Pepper's Lonely Hearts Club Band (Reprise)."

According to biographer Les Norman, the Beatles did not do much LSD while working on what would become Sgt. Pepper's Lonely Hearts Club Band, even though the album was often associated with drug use. John accidentally took a hit of acid one evening while in the studio, thinking it was an upper, and George Martin claimed it was the only time he saw John incapacitated while working in the studio.[72]

In the summer of 1967 the Beatles released the first rock concept album, Sgt. Pepper's Lonely Hearts Club Band.[73] The album went to number one on the UK album chart for 27 weeks, and in the United States, it was the top album for 19 weeks.[74] Within a month of its release, the album had sold half a million copies.

The *Sgt. Pepper's* album cover forged new ground in the world of cover art and pop art. It was a montage of both famous and unknown faces in the midst of flowers, dolls, statues and other artifacts. Images included the Beatles in their younger mop-top days and the Beatles in their Sgt. Pepper costumes, as well as a range of people that in many ways represented the decade. There were movie stars, including Marilyn Monroe and Marlon Brando, writers Edgar Allan Poe and Dylan Thomas, philosophers and scientists including Karl Marx and Albert Einstein, gurus Sri Yukteswar Giri and Sri Paramahansa Yogananda, comedians Laurel and Hardy, dancer Fred Astaire, singer Bob Dylan, psychiatrist Sigmund Freud, among others. John tried to also include images of Jesus Christ and Hitler, but these ideas were later nixed. Printed on the back cover were the lyrics to all the songs on the album, another first. The Beatles won a Grammy award in 1968 for Best Album Cover, Graphic Arts for the *Sgt. Pepper's* cover.

On June 25, 1967, the Beatles recorded a live performance on the BBC television show *Our World*, broadcast live from Studio One at Abbey Road. Three hundred fifty million people tuned in to watch the famous foursome perform "All You Need is Love" to a live audience of celebrities that included Keith Richards and Mick Jagger of the Rolling Stones, Eric Clapton, and Keith Moon of the Who. The studio was filled with flowers and balloons, some spelling out the word "L-O-V-E." Paul wore a red carnation behind his ear as he sang and played guitar. John was clad in a Victorian style coat typical of the Sgt. Pepper time, wearing his trademark round wire-rimmed glasses and chewing gum as he sang into the microphone. The lyrics of the song were purposely simple so that they could be understood by people around the world who were not necessarily fluent in English,[75] and the song was in part a response to some of the issues the world was facing at the time. John included several typically Lennon twists in the song—the trumpets sounding the theme-song of the French Revolution in the opening, and a sarcastic-sounding "She loves you yeah yeah yeah" at the end. The song became an anthem for the Summer of Love.[76]

By this time, John was visibly changed—he was thinner and seemed more somber. People were beginning to become concerned about his health. Drug use affected his appetite, and he was drinking and smoking heavily.[77] There was pressure on the boys to admit that they were using drugs, particularly given what many believed to be drug references in the *Sgt. Pepper's* album, but John remained silent about this to the public. Much to his surprise, however, the typically cautious Paul admitted in a *Life* magazine interview that he had used LSD four times and he shared his enthusiasm that the drug enhanced the creative power of the brain.[78] Public criticism from the British media, American evangelist Billy Graham, and others quickly followed. John and George showed solidarity with Paul by also admitting that they had used acid, but privately John resented that Paul seemed to take the limelight.[79] There was a palpable tension between John and Paul. John felt Paul was trying to take control of the Beatles, and at some level he seemed to become jealous or resentful of Paul's songwriting and attempts to be the leader of the band.[80] But rather than confront Paul with his concerns, John decided to disengage.

TRANSCENDENTAL MEDITATION

George's passion for the sitar and Eastern music developed into an interest in Eastern religion and philosophy, and he began to follow the teachings of the Maharishi Mahesh Yogi. George encouraged the other Beatles to join him practicing transcendental meditation. The Maharishi did not believe in using drugs; instead, he thought that people could experience the same high through meditation. John seemed to like this idea, and Cynthia supported him because she thought it would mean that John would eliminate drugs from his life.[81]

In August 1967, John and Cynthia joined the other Beatles and their partners along with Mick Jagger and his girlfriend, Marianne Faithfull, on a trip to Bangor in north Wales to spend time with the Maharishi. As they departed on the train, Cynthia was carrying luggage and became separated from the others. The train left without her. She stood on the platform and cried. Neil Aspinall, who was not traveling with the Beatles, drove Cynthia to Bangor to catch up with the party, and when she was finally reunited with John, he asked, "Why are you always last, Cyn? How on earth did you manage to miss that train?"[82] He did not seem to notice that she was struggling with the luggage.

When they arrived in Bangor, the Beatles received devastating news. Brian Epstein had been found dead of a suspected drug overdose. By all accounts, John had been largely unaware of Brian's extensive drug use and drinking problems; however, when Brian had checked into a clinic earlier that summer in an effort to kick his substance abuse, John became more aware of the extent of Brian's addiction. John sent him a large floral bouquet with a handwritten note that read "You know I love you . . . I really mean that, John."[83] Brian reportedly burst into tears when he read the note.[84]

Brian had managed the Beatles' for six years, and he had an intense relationship with the boys. He was only 32 years of age at the time of his death. Although John was often publicly mean to Brian, deriding him for being gay and Jewish, he relied on Brian immensely and was clearly devastated by his untimely and unexpected death. When John attempted to give a statement to the press, he appeared ashen in front of the cameras; his usual wittiness was gone and he seemed at an uncharacteristic loss for words:

> "I don't know what to say, you know. We've only just heard and its hard to think of things to say. He's just a beautiful fellow, you know. It's terrible." A reporter asked, "What are your plans now." John replied, "Well we haven't made any yet. We only just heard."[85]

The Maharishi told the boys not to be overwhelmed by grief but to think instead of happy thoughts about Brian because those thoughts would travel to him wherever he was. The boys could not attend the funeral because of the media frenzy their presence was sure to create, so they mourned and dealt with their grief in private.

Brian's death hit John particularly hard. Biographer Albert Goldman wrote that John confessed that he had loved Brian "more than a woman."[86] Biographers, including Les Norman, believe that Brian remained infatuated with John throughout his life and that he never gave up hope that John would return his feelings some day.[87] It is hard to know if John was aware of this, and if it really was what Brian thought, but John certainly suffered as he struggled to move on with his life after yet another unexpected death of someone close to him.

At the time of Brian's death, 17 bottles of pills, including antidepressants and sleeping pills, were found in his house. The results of the inquest into Brian's death ruled that it was accidental, but the Beatles felt guilty nonetheless. After they stopped touring, they had less regular contact with Brian. Since there were no concerts to plan, Brian had less to do for the Beatles, leaving a bit of a void in his life. He worked as a manager for other bands, but they did not have the same relationship with Brian as John, Paul, George, and Ringo did. Brian suffered from depression throughout his life, but he fell into a particularly difficult episode in the weeks before his death. While it is not clear that this had anything to do with the Beatles, the boys still felt bad that they were not aware that their friend was suffering.

The Beatles were not sure what they should do after Brian's death. All they really had done to this point was make music; Brian had been responsible for everything else. Deep down, John was scared about their future.[88] One of their first decisions was to begin Apple Publishing, a company to house all their business affairs in one place. They purchased a building on Savile Row in London, where they established the publishing company in the upstairs, and they opened a clothing boutique in the downstairs space that Pete Shotton was hired to manage. They painted the building with psychedelic colors, and the neighbors complained.

A few days after Brian's death, John wrote to his father suggesting they should get together. Soon after, John's chauffeur met Alf and drove him to Kenwood to see John, who seemed to have a change of heart about his father, perhaps because of his grief over losing Brian, or perhaps because of a letter Alf's brother wrote to John explaining that stories of John's childhood and Alf's departure from England were not quite as Mimi had explained when John was young. John invited Alf to stay at Kenwood. Alf agreed and promptly moved into the servants' quarters where John and Cynthia had lived while the house was being renovated.

Alf was a bit isolated at Kenwood, away from the city and his work. John invited his father's 19-year-old girlfriend, Pauline, to visit. She stayed with John and Cynthia at Kenwood for about three weeks. John was busy working, and so he did not spend much time with them. Pauline helped to watch Julian while they were there so that Cynthia could be with John in London.[89] Then John paid for Alf and Pauline to spend three weeks in Scotland, where they were married. On February 26, 1969, the two had a son together, David Harry Lennon. John bought his father a house in Brighton.

MAGICAL MYSTERY TOUR

Around Christmas 1967, the *Magical Mystery Tour* aired on British television. The film was an unscripted account of the Beatles traveling with ordinary people, including John's uncle Charlie, across the United Kingdom. Modeled in part after American author Ken Kesey and his 1964 travels with the acid-fueled Merry Pranksters across the United States on a bus painted in psychedelic colors, the entourage traveled through locations in the western counties of England where there were ancient burial grounds and storied legends. Paul largely took the lead on the film in Brian's absence, but John did not object and contributed to the planning and creation of the film.[90] John narrated some of the early stages of the story and he had several brief cameo roles in the movie.

The film was the Beatles' first failure, and because it was not successful in the United Kingdom, it never played in the United States. The Beatles released the soundtrack for the television film as an album that met with better success than the show had. It was nominated for a Grammy award for best album in 1968. John contributed to the original music, including the song "I Am the Walrus." John relied in part on Lewis Carroll's poem "The Walrus and the Carpenter" for inspiration, as well as Buddhist and Taoist scriptures for the line "I am he, you are he." The song also incorporates a segment of a dramatic reading from *King Lear* (Act IV, Scene VI) that includes the character Oswald's death scene. This fueled in part some of the public speculation, based on supposed clues in the Beatles lyrics and artwork, suggesting that Paul was dead and had been replaced by a look-alike. The song was the first studio recording after Brian Epstein's death. Lennon later claimed that this was his favorite Beatle song.[91]

In February 1968, the Beatles went to India to spend time at the Maharishi's training center (ashram) in Rishikesh at the foot of the Himalaya mountains on the bank of the Ganges River. The center had low stone cottages with beautiful flowers and shrubs surrounding them. When the Beatles arrived, other celebrities were already there: actress Mia Farrow and her shy sister Prudence (who John later wrote "Dear Prudence" for in an attempt to make her smile),[92] Beach Boy member Mike Love, and the singer Donovan.

The Beatles, clad in Indian attire, meditated for two or three hours before sunrise, and then had a vegetarian breakfast. This was followed by more meditation until noon. They did various chores and work around the center throughout the afternoon. John and Paul often met in the afternoon to write songs together and share new ideas. They wrote approximately 40 new songs during this brief time period. In spite of this creative work, the arrangements in Rishikesh did not interest all the Beatles: Ringo and Maureen went home after 10 days, and Paul and Jane left after a month.

Although John engaged in collaborative work with Paul, he was distant from Cynthia, and any hope she may have had of them becoming closer during this experience was soon dispelled.[93] John blamed their troubles on his effort to engage in meditation, but Cynthia later found out that John was leaving early each morning to go to the post office where he found letters waiting for him from Yoko Ono.

John, Cynthia, George, and Patti left the Maharishi abruptly when Beatles associate Magic Alex (Alex Mardas, head of the Beatles' Apple electronics, who earned his nickname from John) accused the Maharishi of behaving inappropriately with a young American girl. John soon discovered that the Maharishi was exploitative and had planned a deal with ABC television as well as several worldwide centers based on his connections with famous celebrities. When they returned to England, John announced publicly that they had made a mistake.[94] But the time in India was not a total loss. John was drug and alcohol free for several months while they were away, although he started to drink alcohol again on the plane ride back to England,[95] and he had dozens of new songs in the making. Upon their return the Beatles wrote 30 songs over the next two months.

ENTER YOKO

As John and Cynthia settled back into their life at Kenwood, John remained distant from Cynthia. He confessed to her that he had been with other women over the years, but Cynthia told him that it was all right.[96] She had suspected as much, but like many women of her generation had resigned herself to the notion that this was part of life, particularly given the pressures John faced when he was on tour. She accepted it and was always glad that he came back to her. John told her that she was the only one he ever loved, and that he would always love her.

Shortly after this, John suggested that Cynthia take a holiday in Greece with some friends. John was busy writing music for the Beatles' next album, which was originally called *The Beatles*, but after its release became known as the *White Album*. While Cynthia was away, John hung out with his childhood friends John Dunbar and Pete Shotton as he began to use drugs more heavily. At one point John told Pete that he thought he was Jesus Christ. When Pete asked John what he was going to do about that, John replied, "I've got to tell everyone! I've got to let the world know who I am."[97] Pete discouraged him from doing this, warning that people would try to kill him, but John would not listen. At an Apple board meeting the next day, John made the same announcement and insisted on a press release. The others took this in stride, telling John they would need some time to reflect on this before deciding what they would do next.[98]

While Cynthia was away, Yoko came to stay with John at Kenwood. John and Yoko began to work on a recording that later became their album *Unfinished Music No. 1: Two Virgins (with Yoko Ono)*. John asked Pete to help him find a new home for him and Yoko. He confessed to his childhood friend that he was completely in love with her. He did not care about money, the Beatles, or anything else. Instead, he explained:

I'll go and live with her in a f***ing *tent* if I have to . . . It's just like how we used to fall in love when we were kids . . . when you'd meet a girl and you'd think about her and want to be with her all the time, how your mind was just filled with her? Well Yoko's upstairs now, and I can't wait to get back to her.[99]

Pete stood by his long-time friend, and he even took Yoko shopping for clothes at John's request.

When Cynthia returned, she found Yoko settled comfortably into Kenwood. Cynthia was in a state of shock and went to a friend's house for a few days. When she returned, John acted as though nothing had happened. He told Cynthia, "It's you I love, Cyn . . . I love you now more than ever before."[100] Everything seemed to return to normal for a few days as John and Cynthia resumed their old routines and spent time talking.

Soon after this, John and Paul decided to go to New York on a business trip for Apple. John did not wish for Cynthia to join him, so she went to Italy for two weeks, taking her mother and Julian along for company. Cynthia had been to Pesaro once before with her mother and Julian when John was on tour, and she spent a great deal of time in the hotel, sheltered by the Bassanini family who owned it.[101] When she returned, they stayed once again with the Bassanini family, and on this trip, Cynthia met Roberto Bassanini, the son of the hotel owners. One night Cynthia went out on the town with Roberto, and when she returned, Magic Alex was waiting for her. Alex had a message from John: he wanted a divorce, and he was going to assume custody of Julian.

Cynthia fell ill. Newspapers had pictures of John and Yoko on the cover. Their first public outing was to see Victor Spinetti's play adaptation of John's book *In His Own Write*. As the two entered the theater, the press snapped pictures of them and yelled questions asking where Cynthia was. It was clear the marriage was over. When Cynthia returned to London, divorce papers arrived. John accused Cynthia of adultery with Roberto Bassanini.

At first, John allowed Cynthia and Julian to move back to Kenwood while he took a flat in London with Yoko. Paul was the only member of the Beatles establishment to visit Cynthia after John left. George and Ringo seemed to keep their distance, perhaps out of loyalty to or fear of John.[102] Paul wrote a song for Julian that he initially titled "Hey Jules." Later he renamed it "Hey Jude." Paul's life was also turned a bit upside down at the time. Jane Asher found Paul with another woman, and she ended their five-year relationship.[103] Paul was clearly heartbroken, and he knew that the split was his fault. A few months later, he met an

American photographer named Linda Eastman. Things were definitely changing for the John and the other Beatles.

NOTES

1. Geoffrey Giuliano, *Blackbird: The Life and Times of Paul McCartney* (New York: DeCapo Press, 1997), p. 81.

2. Elizabeth Thomson and David Gutman, *The Lennon Companion: Twenty-Five Years of Comment* (New York: Schirmer Books, 1987), p. 71.

3. Ibid., p. 74.

4. Albert Goldman, *The Lives of John Lennon* (New York: William Morrow and Company, 1988), p. 191.

5. Philip Norman, *John Lennon: The Life* (New York: Harper Collins Publishers, 2008), p. 386.

6. Cynthia Lennon, *John* (New York: Crown Publishers, 2005), p. 168.

7. Norman, p. 409.

8. Ibid.

9. Ibid.

10. May Pang and Henry Edwards, *Loving John* (New York: Warner Bros, 1983), p. 31.

11. Norman, p. 410.

12. Ibid.

13. Ibid.

14. Olivier Julien, *Sgt. Pepper and the Beatles: It Was Forty Years Ago Today* (Hampshire, England: Ashgate Publishing, 2008), p. 3.

15. Paul later purchased this letter as a gift for Julian.

16. Lennon, n.p. (photo image).

17. Ibid., p. 170.

18. In 1917, King George V established a British order of chivalry called the Most Excellent Order of the British Empire. The motto of this order is "For God and the Empire," and it has the largest membership of any British order, hosting five classifications: Knight or Dame Grand Cross (GBE), Knight or Dame Commander (KBE or DBE), Commander (CBE), Officer (OBE), and Member (MBE), which is the lowest rank in the order.

19. Lennon, p. 173.

20. Hunter Davies, *The Beatles* (New York: McGraw Hill Publishing, 1985), p. 201.

21. Elizabeth Partridge, *John Lennon: All I Want Is the Truth* (New York: Viking Press, 2005), p. 115.

22. Lennon, p. 175.

23. Davies, p. 208.

24. Lennon, p. 178.

25. Ibid.

26. Norman, p. 380.

27. Ibid.

28. Goldman, p. 288.

29. Lennon, p. 180.

30. Norman, p. 422.

31. Lennon, p. 182.

32. Norman, p. 426.

33. Lennon, p. 185.

34. Partridge, p. 117.

35. Ibid.

36. Goldman, p. 198.

37. Norman, p. 402.

38. See Jane Wright, "The Beatles' Movie Magic Chart Band's Rise and Fall," *Liverpool Daily Post*, August, 31, 2009, http://www.liverpooldailypost.co.uk/liverpool-life-features/liverpool-arts/2009/08/31/the-beatles-movie-magic-92534-24568052/ (accessed September 1, 2009).

39. Thomson and Gutman, p. 72.

40. Norman, p. 441.

41. Goldman, 1988.

42. Thomson and Gutman, p. 80.

43. Geoff Emerick, *Here There and Everywhere: My Life Recording with the Beatles* (New York: Gotham Books, 2006).

44. Ibid.

45. Lennon, p. 189.

46. Ibid., p. 190.

47. Norman, p. 447.

48. Ibid., p. 450.

49. Norman, p. 451.

50. Strongman and Parker, p. 83.

51. Ibid., p. 83.

52. On November 22, 2008, the Vatican's newspaper issued a statement forgiving Lennon for declaring that the Beatles were more famous than Jesus Christ.

53. Norman, p. 453.

54. Davies, p. 212.

55. Goldman, p. 207.

56. Norman, p. 432.

57. Davies, p. 284.

58. Partridge, p. 123.

59. Strongman and Parker believe this is when Lennon first came to the attention of the FBI and CIA in the United States.

60. Thomson and Gutman, p. 129.

61. Norman, p. 457.

62. Clips from the movie *How I Won the War* can be found on You Tube.com.

63. Happenings were performances that were considered as art and that purposely intended to break down the barrier between artist and viewer, making the audience part of the art.

64. Goldman, pp. 242–43.

65. Ibid.

66. Davies, p. 290.

67. Julien, p. 5.

68. Lucy died September 22, 2009, after suffering from lupus. Julian was in touch with her before her death, and he released a single titled "Lucy" in December 2009 to honor her.

69. Robertson, p. 69.

70. Robertson points out that John could have changed his story about this song years later when the connection to drugs could have brought renewed publicity to the song and less public concern about the connection to drugs, but he never did.

71. Geoffrey Giuliano and Brenda Giuliano, *The Lost Lennon Interviews* (Holbrook, MA: Adams Media Corporation, 1996), p. 38.

72. Norman, p. 492.

73. Some claim this remains the best concept album more than 40 years later. See Strongman and Parker.

74. The album is still listed in the number one position on *Rolling Stone's* list of the 500 Greatest Albums of All Time. *Revolver* is in the

number three position, *Rubber Soul* is fifth, and *The Beatles (The White Album)* is 10th.

75. Robertson, p. 71.

76. Goldman, p. 264.

77. Lennon, p. 195.

78. Norman, p. 498.

79. Ibid., p. 499.

80. Goldman, p. 249.

81. Lennon, p. 196.

82. Ibid., p. 198.

83. Norman, p. 504.

84. Ibid.

85. See television news coverage of Lennon's comments after Brian Epstein's death, captured in *Bob Smeaton, The Beatles Anthology,* DVD, produced by Neil Aspinall and Chips Chipperfield (London; Apple Corps., 1995).

86. Goldman, p. 245.

87. Norman, p. 502.

88. Ibid.

89. Goldman, p. 291.

90. Norman, p. 517.

91. Robertson, p. 74.

92. Strongman and Parker, p. 14.

93. Lennon, p. 209.

94. Goldman, p. 296.

95. Ibid., p. 298.

96. Lennon, p. 211.

97. Goldman, p. 301.

98. Ibid., p. 302.

99. Ibid., p. 303.

100. Lennon, p. 218.

101. Ibid., p. 189.

102. Norman, p. 546.

103. Ibid.

Chapter 6

JOHN AND YOKO

I don't believe in the Beatles, that's all. I don't believe in the Beatles myth . . . It was a dream. I don't believe in the dream anymore.

—*John Lennon, 1970*[1]

Cynthia and Julian remained at Kenwood, and John and Yoko moved into Ringo's flat on Montagu Square in Marleybone, London, where Jimi Hendrix formerly lived. The couple spent the summer of 1968 secluded in the basement apartment, using drugs and living in what most people would describe as squalor.[2] Dirty clothes, newspapers, and magazines cluttered the floor, but the couple did not seem to mind. They were in love, experiencing what John later described as "a strange cocktail of love, sex, and forgetfulness."[3]

Although Yoko Ono was already well known in New York and some international circles, few in England knew who she was. Her affiliation with the Fluxus group,[4] an international network of artists whose work blended various media and disciplines, did not generate a great deal of attention in Britain. Yoko first came into the public eye in England with her avant-garde art exhibits and the release of her film *Bottoms*, which consisted of close-ups of men and women's buttocks as they

walked naked on a treadmill and spoke out loud about the experience.
Her work stirred some measure of controversy, but John thought it was
hilarious and believed it confirmed her genius.[5] From their first days
together, John became enthralled with filmmaking. The couple created
short avant-garde films, the first two of which were shot during one afternoon at John's home in Kenwood. Film No. 5, also known as *Smile*,
is a 52-minute close-up of John's face as he makes different expressions.
It was screened at the Chicago Film Festival in 1968, where half the
audience members left after the first half-hour of viewing.[6] The second
film, *Two Virgins*, captured images of John and Yoko's faces as the two
are fused together.

Soon all of Britain and the world recognized Yoko Ono as she appeared on the arm of her famous boyfriend, John Lennon. One of their
first public appearances as a couple was at the opening of *The John
Lennon Play: In His Own Write* at the Old Vic Theatre on Waterloo
Road in London. The one-act production, directed by Victor Spinetti,
was based on John's books *In His Own Write* (1964) and *A Spaniard
in the Works* (1965). John's attendance on opening night with Yoko
stirred more interest among the press than did the play itself. Photographers shouted out, "Where's your wife?" as the two entered the theater,
but the best reply that the usually witty John could offer was "I don't
know."[7]

The British public was generally not kind to Yoko. Girls who waited
for John outside the Abbey Road Studio and other places he frequented
yelled at Yoko, calling her names like "chink" and "yellow." One person pushed a bunch of yellow roses into Yoko's hands stem first, intentionally injuring her with the thorns.[8] Yoko did not receive a warm
welcome from John's family and friends either. Aunt Mimi in particular
did not hide her feelings about Yoko to John. When John took Yoko to
meet her, Mimi asked "Who's the poisoned dwarf, John?"[9] She tried to
warn John that his relationship with Yoko would affect his popularity
with the British public, but John shrugged off her concerns. Yoko had
endured difficult times as a child in Tokyo during and after the war,
and she seemed to manage these feelings of animosity toward her fairly
well.[10]

As their relationship grew, John began to take Yoko to recording
sessions with the Beatles. Up to this time, the studio had always been

a fairly insular place for the boys to work, and none of them had ever taken women into the studio; instead, they expected their wives to be at home looking after things while they were away, as was the norm during this time period. Although Paul, George, and Ringo were not impressed with Yoko's presence, they did not say too much because they expected John would soon tire of her and she would be gone.[11] But they guessed wrong, and Yoko remained. Worse yet for them, she whispered in John's ear during studio sessions and produced random sounds as they recorded. Yoko's presence soon created a great deal of stress for all the Beatles as well as their producer, George Martin, who felt inhibited with her in the studio.[12] The boys had always been able to openly criticize one another in the studio and to speak frankly with Martin to move a project along, but now they felt constrained and seemed to resent that John responded to Yoko's suggestions rather than to their own.[13] Even Paul, who understood what it felt like to be in love (he was deeply in love with American photographer Linda Eastman at the time), could not understand why Yoko had to constantly be at John's side, even when John and Paul were trying to write songs. As tension mounted, Ringo, who was known to be the most easy-going of them all, quit the band because he was fed up with how things were going. Fortunately, the others convinced him to rejoin them a week later—they had recording obligations to fulfill.

The Beatles were not the only people who seemed to be baffled by John's attraction to Yoko, and people today still puzzle over their unlikely union. Biographer Les Norman claims that Yoko fulfilled an ideal for John—she was an artist unlike any other he had encountered since Stu Sutcliffe, and she fulfilled his vision of an ideal woman who was beautiful, intelligent, a "dark-eyed Oriental," and his equal.[14] John believed Yoko fell in love with him for who he was, not because he was a Beatle; indeed she claimed that when they first met, she had no idea who he was and she was not really aware of the Beatles. She was a woman who insisted on equality in their relationship, and she was clearly different than other women he had known.[15] The couple became inseparable, taking meals and even bathroom breaks together. Some thought it was evidence of Yoko's control over John that she went everywhere with him, but Yoko explained that it was really John's jealousy and fear that if Yoko was left alone while he took a break at the studio, for example, she might go off with one of the other Beatles.[16] She claimed that John was jealous of anyone who might take Yoko's attention away from him.[17]

THE *WHITE ALBUM*

In spite of significant tension among the Beatles because of Yoko as well as added pressures surrounding Apple Corps,[18] John continued to write new songs and further develop the work he began in India. He contributed these songs to the *White Album*, the unofficial name of a double album with a plain white cover that simply read "The Beatles." The album was a potpourri of musical styles that reflected individual band members' own interests rather than the more collaborative writing they had engaged in the past.

The album took nearly five months to complete as the Beatles worked tirelessly in the studio. They began the sessions by recording two versions of the song "Revolution." The song was satirical and made fun of middle-class youth who called for revolution but did not really understand their own position of privilege in relation to the forces of oppression in the world.[19] The first version of "Revolution," known at "Revolution 1" was performed at a slow tempo, and the original recording lasted 10 minutes. Only the first four minutes of this recording made it onto the album. Paul and George added "shoo-be-doo-wahs" in the background as John sang lead. Yoko added random sounds and comments like "you become naked" throughout the recording.

John was not satisfied with this version of the song, so he took the remaining six minutes of the original recording and turned it into the second version, "Revolution (No. 9)." This version was a sound collage at a faster tempo, and the changes in the song compared to "Revolution 1" suggested sounds of violence and chaos that would happen during a revolution. Both versions had different statements about John's commitment to "Revolution." In the version released on a single, John claimed, "when you talk about destruction you can count me out," while in the second version he claimed he could be counted in. John later explained that he made a mistake by doing this and the song that came out was really antirevolution. He explained this indecision in relation to his personal fear of violence and his own ignorance:

I didn't want to get killed. I didn't really know that much about the Maoists, but I just knew that they seemed to be so few and yet they painted themselves green and stood in front of the police waiting to get picked off . . . I thought the original Communist revolutionaries coordinated themselves a bit better and didn't go around shooting about it. That was how I felt—I was really asking a question.[20]

The recording was completed when Paul was in the United States on holiday, and when he heard the final version he did not like it. Neither did many of the Beatles' fans; in fact, it is the least popular of all Beatles sound recordings,[21] although a version of it appeared on the flipside of the popular single "Hey Jude."

John's original contributions to the *White Album* were diverse. "Goodnight" was a children's song, a lullaby written for Julian, which contrasted with the self-mocking rock tune "Glass Onion." In British slang, glass onion means a monocle, and in the song, John makes references to the Beatles' earlier tunes. John also contributed the blues-rock number "Yer Blues," which contained suicidal lyrics that began "I'm lonely, want to die." John's song "Dear Prudence," written for Mia Farrow's sister in India, was recorded with complex three-part harmonies against more stabbing guitar sounds, and it features Paul on drums since it was recorded during the time Ringo took a break from the band. John also included "Julia," a poignant and sad song in memory of his mother. John sings alone with an acoustic guitar, the only time he commands a full solo performance on a Beatles album.

One of John's more brilliant songs appeared on this album: "Happiness Is a Warm Gun." The title came from the cover of an American gun magazine that read: "Happiness Is a Warm Gun in Your Hand." The song had vocals that at times sounded like a throw-back to the 1950s, but the tempos changed frequently, and the electric guitars contributed sounds that were at times fuzzy, and other times clear. The lyrics were metaphorical and full of sexual symbolism, including the line "Mother Superior jump the gun," an early reference to John's nickname for Yoko.[22]

Paul contributed "Martha My Dear," which featured piano and a brass band; "Ob-La-Di, Ob-La-Da," which shows the influence and rising popularity of reggae in England; and "Blackbird," a song written about the rising racial tensions in the United States. John and Paul came together on songs like "Helter Skelter," and John contributed saxophone to the recording. George continued to make progress as a songwriter, contributing "Piggies," complete with animal sound effects that John invented using tape loops, and "While My Guitar Gently Weeps," which included Eric Clapton on lead guitar.

The album debuted at number one on the British charts, and within three weeks it also was the top album on the American charts. The album was filled with oblique messages, like "the walrus was Paul," and fans were enthralled as they searched through the album's sound and lyrics for what they believed would be hidden messages of advice from the band. The eclectic nature of the music brought mixed reviews, but the album remains one of the best in the history of rock music.

LIFE AS ART, LIFE AS TRIAL

In the late 1960s, John became more actively involved with the art world. On June 15, 1968, John and Yoko had permission to engage living art through John's conceptualization of the Acorn Event as part of the National Sculpture Exhibition. During the event, they planted two acorns, one toward the East and the other toward the West, to serve as a symbol of their union as well as a message of hope and spiritual growth. It was clear through this event that John understood how concepts were as powerful, if not more so, than objects.[23]

In July, John and Yoko opened an exhibit of John's work at the Robert Fraser Gallery, complete with an upturned hat on the ground to accept tips and a handwritten sign that read "for the artist." John dedicated the exhibit, called "You Are Here," to Yoko with love, but while her influence was evident, the displays primarily reflected John's childhood. The name of the exhibit was inspired by Liverpool's parks, which had maps with the phrase "You Are Here" on them. One display was of charity collection boxes that were common in John's childhood as orphanages and other causes tried to collect money for the needy. Other displays were more whimsical in nature, with various drawings and messages.

John and Yoko opened the show with the release of 365 helium balloons, each containing a small note asking the finder to write back to

John. As responses to the helium balloons came in from across England, the couple began to realize the public's disapproval of them. Many contained disparaging comments. The two did not seem to mind too much; instead, they considered themselves to be works of art in their own right.[24]

John began to provide financial backing for Yoko's art exhibits. *The Half a Wind Show* opened at the Lisson Gallery in North London on John's 27th birthday with a display that consisted of a room full of furniture that was cut in half. John contributed to the exhibit with an idea about including bottles that were also cut in half. At the last minute, John took his name from the poster advertising the show, and he replaced it with the word "Me," so the show was credited to "Yoko and Me." John reportedly did not visit the show once it opened.[25]

Yoko became pregnant by John in September 1968, which complicated his plans to divorce Cynthia on charges of adultery. Once Cynthia learned of Yoko's pregnancy, she proceeded to sue John. The two were officially divorced on November 8, 1968. The settlement included £100,000 to Cynthia and £2,400 annually for Julian's support. John also placed £100,000 in a trust for Julian to access when he turned 21. The money would be completely Julian's, provided John had no more children; otherwise, the money would be split evenly among his children. Cynthia assumed full custody of their son, and John saw him only infrequently after the divorce.

Although John was now single, he was not free to marry Yoko because she was still married to an American named Tony Cox, the father of their daughter Kyoko. To move these divorce proceedings along, John paid Yoko's joint debts with Tony, which amounted to £100,000.[26] Their divorce was finalized January 30, 1969, but Tony and Yoko could not come to agreement about Kyoko's custody. John wanted Yoko to give up custody of her daughter, but Yoko would not agree.[27] This unresolved arrangement created a great deal of trouble for the couple over the next several years.

More problems soon followed. On October 18, police raided John and Yoko's flat at Montagu Square, searching for drugs. John had advance warning that the police were coming, but even though he thought he had cleaned the apartment of any incriminating evidence, police still found a small amount of marijuana, approximately half an ounce. John and Yoko were arrested, and John pled guilty to drug possession in an attempt to keep Yoko from being deported. He was fined £150 plus £21 for court costs. John also was given due warning that he would be sentenced to prison if he was caught again. The couple was evicted from the Montagu flat and returned to Kenwood where they took up residence in a bedroom.

A few weeks after their arrest, Yoko miscarried after six months of pregnancy. John remained by her side at the hospital, sleeping on the floor and recording the fetus's final heartbeats. Yoko later claimed that the miscarriage was instigated because John beat her.[28] They named the unborn child John Ono Lennon II, and buried him in a small casket in an undisclosed location.[29]

As the Beatles finished the *White Album*, John and Yoko released their debut album, which they called *Unfinished Music No. 1: Two Virgins (with Yoko Ono)*, the second release under the Apple records label. The record contained tape loops that consist of John playing different musical instruments while trying out various sound effects, something he had been doing in his home recording studio for more than two years. It was an adventure in the avant-garde the two began on their first evening together at Kenwood. At first Peter Brown at Apple thought the album was a joke; when he realized it was not, he tried to talk John out of making it public. Perhaps even more shocking than the music was the album cover. On the front cover, John and Yoko stood facing the camera, totally naked. The backside of the album showed the nude couple standing with their backside to the camera. John later explained, "We used the straightest, most unflattering picture just to show that we were human . . . People are always looking at people like me, trying to see some secret. 'What do they do? Do they go to the bathroom? Do they eat?' so we just said 'Here.'"[30] The album received negative responses from Sir Joseph Lockwood (the EMI chairman), Paul McCartney, and others across Britain. Aunt Mimi was appalled, and public's general response was "Yuck!"[31] When the album was released in the United States, it was seized by customs in New Jersey, and a trial for obscenity followed. The few albums that were eventually sold in the United States were wrapped in brown covers.

At the end of the year, John and Yoko appeared with young Julian Lennon at the Rolling Stones' *Rock and Roll Circus*, a television special modeled after the Beatles' *Magical Mystery Tour*. The event was filmed in a big top circus tent with other celebrity rock and rollers, including Jethro Tull, The Who, Marianne Faithfull, and Taj Mahal. John and Mick Jagger engaged in a short parody during a break in the music. The two old friends exchanged a few one-liners as John, tongue-in-cheek, played the role of a television interviewer, and John told Mick, "I want to hold your man." Most significantly perhaps, John had a stage debut without the three other Beatles, belting out "Yer Blues" with Keith Richards, Eric Clapton, violinist Ivry Gitlist, and percussionist Mitch Mitchell from the Jimi Hendrix Experience as part of an impromptu one-time group he called the Dirty Mac. John seemed to enjoy the experience, dancing in the stands as Jagger captured the audience with riveting performances of "Jumping Jack Flash" and "Sympathy for the Devil." Unfortunately, the Stones did not like the recording and could not resolve differences over how they would be paid, so they blocked its release for 30 years.[32]

In spite of his public persona, as New Year's Eve 1968 approached, these had not been particularly happy times for Lennon. He was struggling with heroin addiction, his public image was damaged, and his relationships with the other Beatles and EMI were in trouble.[33] Once he made a commitment to Yoko, he seemed to be embroiled in one problem after another. The music John wrote during this time expressed the rage and pain he experienced.

BUSINESS AND FINANCIAL PROBLEMS

On January 2, 1969, the Beatles met as Paul attempted to bring the group together after the *White Album*. Paul proposed doing an album and documentary, but the others nixed his ideas. Yoko continued to contribute to the tension among the group, and the boys bickered quite a bit. George threatened to quit, but then he learned by chance that pianist Billy Preston was in town. George invited him into the studio hoping this would bring the creative energy the Beatles needed. It turned out George was right—when Preston was in the studio, the boys seemed to get along well, and they produced some of their best work. The Beatles relocated to a new studio space designed by Magic Alex Mardas in the basement of 3 Savile Road, where they continued to complete their album. The recordings from this time became known as the Get Back Sessions.

On Thursday, January 30, a cold and drab day in London, the Beatles went to the roof at Savile Row where amps were set up. Ringo wore a shiny red plastic coat, which contrasted with John's brown fur coat. The Beatles, accompanied by Billy Preston on keyboards, began to perform as cameras rolled. They belted out "Don't Let Me Down," "I've Got a Feeling," "One after 909," and "Dig a Pony." The police came and asked them to stop because local office workers were complaining about the noise, but they negotiated to play one last song, wrapping up the performance with "Get Back." As they finished and took off their guitars, Paul said "Thanks Mo," in reference to Maureen Starkey's applause, and John commented:

I'd like to say thanks on behalf of the group and ourselves—and I hope we passed the audition.[34]

The performance lasted 42 minutes. It was the last time the Beatles performed together in public.

A few weeks later, John declared the band was financially broke and he was down to his last £50,000, even though there were estimates that they earned as much as $154 million.[35] After Brian Epstein's death, Linda Eastman's brother John managed the band. John Lennon did not like this arrangement, and so he turned to Allen Klein, who began to manage his and Yoko's work. Klein had a reputation for being tough. John arranged a meeting with Klein, John Eastman, Lee Eastman (John and Linda's father), and Paul. Klein discovered in advance of the meeting that Lee Eastman's name had been Leopold Epstein until he changed it after graduating from Harvard, and so throughout the meeting, John kept calling Lee Eastman "Epstein," angering him until he stormed out.[36] From this moment on, the rift between Paul and John deepened. In spite of his reservations, Paul did, however, agree to let Klein investigate the Beatles' finances. Klein discovered how poorly Brian Epstein had managed their fortune, and he confirmed that the group was indeed financially broke.

The Beatles' primary source of income was through record sales. The boys never renegotiated their original contract with EMI, and they were only earning about 6 cents for each $5 or $6 album they sold. By record industry standards at that time, they really should have been earning 50 cents per album.[37] EMI was certainly benefiting financially from the band's successes. In 1968 the recording company's earnings increased 80 percent due to the Beatles' popularity. Even though the Beatles signed with Capitol Records in 1968 and increased their earnings to 40 cents per album, this was still inadequate. They attempted to expand Apple Corps into other commercial ventures. They tried to support other artists and even discussed the possibility of beginning a school for children, but this never was realized. They did succeed in opening a clothing boutique, but this was short-lived. The Beatles closed the clothing boutique in August 1968. The venture ended up costing them £112,000 in stock, building renovations, and fall clothing merchandise.

The Beatles did not make much money through their songwriting. When Brian Epstein first began to manage the Beatles, their music publishing was handled through Northern Songs Ltd. For each song published, Dick James at Northern received 50 percent, and the other 50 percent was split between John, Paul, and Brian Epstein (20-20-10). John and Paul provided Northern with music through their own company, Lenmac Enterprises Ltd., which they sold to Northern for £140,000 each. They then founded a subpublishing company called Maclen, Inc.,[38] 20 percent of which was owned by Apple, and they agreed to provide Northern with songs through 1973. Royalties and world-wide radio playing rights poured into Northern as their music was bought and listened to around the world.

The Beatles' tours were poorly negotiated, which caused another source of financial strain. Tour promoter Arthur Howes, hired by Brian Epstein, retained 50 percent of the tour revenues in England. In the United States, the band had a 60/40 split once they earned $25,000, but this should have been renegotiated to benefit them more. Movies generated about $15,000 per person for the first film, but these eventually increased to $7–$8 million for their first two films between 1964 and 1980. Taxes were high in Britain, and the Beatles paid as much as 94 percent of their earnings in taxes.[39] Because of this, they sought tax shelters so that they could hold onto more of what they earned, and they invested in business ventures through Apple Corps.

Allen Klein finally determined the bottom line to be £78,000 net income for the Beatles in 1968. Of this, John owed Apple £64,000; Paul owed £66,000; and George and Ringo each owed £135,0000. In May, Allen Klein officially became the Beatles' manager. He had John, George, and Ringo's support, but not Paul's. Paul wanted his father-in-law, John Eastman, to be the band's official manager, but he was out-voted by the others. Klein's first responsibility was to renegotiate the Beatles' contract with EMI. He also eliminated the various projects at Apple that were not profitable, such as Apple films and the Apple school, and he fired any staff he thought were no longer needed. Klein seemed unconcerned that some of the staff thought they were personal friends.

In March 1969, Dick James sold 23 percent of Northern Songs to Lew Grade. At the time, Northern had 129 Lennon-McCartney tunes and was ranked among the top companies on the London Stock Exchange. James did not tell John and Paul in advance of the sale. Allen Klein struck a delicate deal to give John and Paul the majority, and in the process found out that Paul had already increased his holdings in the company without letting John know. When the meeting was held to seal the final deal, John lost his temper and stormed out. Sir Lew Grade and ATV music secured control of Northern Songs.[40]

MARRIAGE AND PEACE

On March 14, 1969, in the midst of these extensive business and financial woes, John decided that he wished to marry Yoko immediately. Paul married Linda Eastman just two days earlier, and it is difficult to know how much his sense of competition with Paul fueled the sudden plans to marry. John first tried to marry Yoko on a boat on the English Channel, but when this could not be arranged, he flew Yoko to Paris. They spent four days in Paris before flying to Gibraltar to be married. The bride and groom were both clad in white for the ceremony.

From Gibraltar, the newlyweds went to Amsterdam. Here they used the publicity generated from their marriage to promote world peace by engaging a bed-in in room 902 of the Amsterdam Hilton Hotel. The press clambered to the scene when it was announced there would be something happening during John and Yoko's honeymoon, but rather

Beatle John Lennon waves his marriage certificate as his bride, Japanese artist Yoko Ono, stands at his side after their wedding at the Rock of Gibraltar on March 20, 1969. They are about to board a chartered jet to Paris for their honeymoon. (AP Photo.)

than finding John and Yoko naked in bed as many expected, particularly after the release of the *Two Virgins* album, they found them clad in traditional looking pajamas, claiming they would stay in bed for a week to protest violence in the world.

There had been a lot of violence in the world in the year leading up to John and Yoko's marriage, and John's quest for peace was framed largely as an effort to eliminate violence.[41] In the United States, the civil rights movement experienced significant loss when Martin Luther King, Jr. was assassinated and U.S. Senator Robert F. Kennedy was murdered during his campaign to become president. The Vietnam War raged on, and the world was still reeling from the violence of the Tet Offensive, the My Lai massacre, and other horrors that resulted in thousands of lost lives and many more casualties. German Josef Bachman fired three gunshots into left-wing leader Rudi Dutschke's head in an assassination attempt. Feminist Valerie Solanas, who believed in male gendercide and wished to create an all-female society, shot and wounded artist Andy Warhol as he entered his studio. In Czecho-slovakia, Alexander Dubcek established a Prague Spring, a period of political liberation, which ended when Warsaw Pact troops and tanks invaded the country in August. In Mexico, a student demonstration ended in a bloodbath at La Plaza de las Tres Culturas in Tlatelolco just 10 days before the summer Olympics were set to begin. There were also violent uprisings in Ireland, Paris, and China, and the enormity of it all was certainly difficult to understand.

The bed-in embodied John's philosophy of "life as art and art as life."[42] John finally felt that he was able to speak out politically, some-thing Brian Epstein had discouraged him from doing when the Beatles were touring. John knew his public image was suffering, and he hoped the bed-ins could help to recreate his and Yoko's public image in a more positive way. Some among the press bought it, but some did not. The more cynical members of the press dubbed the pair "Joko" and called them self-indulgent.[43] John seemed to be demonstrating against violence as much as he was demonstrating for peace.[44] John hoped the bed-ins would inspire young people to protest in nonviolent ways, ex-plaining that "violence begets violence, and the establishment knows how to fight violence, but they don't know how to fight candy. We just want to tell them here's an instance of how to protest by staying bed."[45] He understood the contradictions between his public commitment to peace and his own personal struggles with violence, particularly against women. Years later he admitted:

> I was a hitter. I couldn't express myself, and I hit. I fought men and I hit women. That is why I am always on about peace, you see. It is the most violent people who go for love and peace. I will have to be a lot older before I can face in public how I treated women as a youngster.[46]

After Amsterdam, the newlyweds went to Vienna where they met reporters in a white bag fashioned from a bed cover. The phenomenon of speaking while enclosed in the cloth bag became known as Bag-ism. John and Yoko intended to satirize prejudice and stereotyping by demonstrating that no one could be judged based on skin color, gender, or some other factor if they were in a bag because they could only be

Beatle John Lennon and his
wife, Yoko Ono, hold a bed-in
for peace in Room 902, the
presidential suite at the
Hilton Hotel in Amsterdam
on March 25, 1969. The
newlyweds, holding solitary
tulips, began the seven-day
bed-in to protest against war.
(AP Photo.)

heard and not seen. They referred to the practice as total communication because the listener had to focus primarily on the message, not the
messenger.

Soon after John and Yoko were wed, John changed his name to John
Winston Ono Lennon during a ceremony reaffirming their commitment to one another atop Apple studio in front of the commissioner
of oaths.[47] It demonstrated in part John's love for Yoko and his growing
understanding of her feminist beliefs—she was willing to change her
name for him, and he was willing to change his name for her.[48] When
John and Yoko's names were combined, there were now nine O's in
their names, John's favorite number. John explained at a 1969 press
conference that Yoko "released" him and "I'm me again. I got lost in the
Beatles, and now it's John Lennon again. That's what she's done."[49]

After they were married, John continued to write and record music.
He wrote "The Ballad of John and Yoko" about their honeymoon adventures, recording the song in an afternoon session with Paul. George

and Ringo were away, so the two doubled on instruments—John on lead guitar and lead vocal, Paul on drums, bass, piano, and maracas. John and Yoko also continued their creative collaborations, releasing *Unfinished Music No. 2: Life with the Lions (With Yoko Ono)*—John's favorite childhood radio show was *Life with the Lyons*. Zapple, a subsidiary label of Apple, released the album in May. It contained more of John and Yoko's experimental music as well as the sound of the heartbeat of the baby they had lost a few months earlier. Of course it did not get much radio play, and John complained that Apple did not do enough to promote the album.

In May, the couple planned to sail to the United States on the *Queen Elizabeth 2*, but Lennon's visa to the United States was denied because of his drug conviction. Instead, the Lennons flew to the Bahamas, and then to Toronto, where they settled into the Queen Elizabeth Hotel in Montreal for their second bed-in for peace. They talked with approximately 150 press people daily, and they called more than 350 radio stations in the United States. When a reporter asked what John was hoping to accomplish, he spontaneously replied, "All we are saying is give peace a chance." The phrase stuck, and John wrote the song "Give Peace A Chance" from his bed in Montreal, performing it live as visitors who ranged from the press to famous celebrities like Timothy Leary and Allen Ginsberg sang along. The song, which was the first solo single released by a Beatle while the band was still together, climbed the charts to number 2 in England and number 14 in the United States almost as soon as it was released. Even though Paul had nothing to do with the song, John credited it to Lennon-McCartney as he did all his former songs. John later expressed regret that he had not given credit to Yoko, who he noted was really his co-author on the piece.[50] The song quickly became an anthem for the antiwar movement in the United States. Approximately half a million people, led by folk singer Pete Seeger, sang it during a war protest in Washington, DC, on October 15, 1969.

John had clearly begun to create his own path separately from the Beatles, and while his obligations with this group that made him world famous were not yet complete, he was gaining confidence that he could go it alone. The public and his family and friends seemed to be watching with mixed reactions that ranged from disgust to adulation. With

Yoko at his side, John recreated his public image and his private life, challenging social norms and daring others to do the same.

NOTES

1. Geoffrey Giuliano and Brenda Giuliano, *The Lost Lennon Interviews* (Holbrook, MA: Adams Media Corporation, 1996), p. 233.

2. Albert Goldman, *The Lives of John Lennon* (New York: William Morrow and Company, 1988), p. 311.

3. Ibid.

4. The work *fluxus* is from the Latin word meaning "to flow." The Fluxus group's origins are often credited to American composer John Cage's experimental music in the 1950s, but the network was named and organized by Lithuanian George Maciunas, whose Fluxus manifesto, written in 1963, urged readers to "purge the world of bourgeois sickness, 'intellectual', professional & commercialized culture . . . PROMOTE A REVOLUTIONARY FLOOD AND TIDE IN ART, . . . promote NON ART REALITY to be grasped by all peoples, not only critics, dilettantes and professionals. . . . FUSE the cadres of cultural, social & political revolutionaries into united front & action" (George Maciunus, Manifesto, 1963, http://www.artnotart.com/fluxus/gmaciunas-manifesto.html [accessed April 17, 2010]). Other early associates with this Dada-inspired avant-garde group included performance artist and sculptor Joseph Beuys, visual and sound artist Nam June Paik, composer La Monte Young, composer and poet Dick Higgins, and painter and sculptor Wolf Vostell. Yoko Ono was among the early members, and her experiments with performance art, poetry, and film reflected this affiliation.

5. Goldman, p. 270.

6. See John Lennon and Yoko Ono's Filmography, http://homepage.ntlworld.com/carousel/pob15.html (accessed April 17, 2010).

7. See John Lennon and Yoko Ono's Filmography, http://homepage.ntlworld.com/carousel/pob17.html (accessed April 17, 2010).

8. Philip Norman, *John Lennon: The Life* (New York: Harper Collins Publishers, 2008), p. 557.

9. Ibid., p. 559.

10. Ibid., p. 558.

11. Ibid., p. 553.

12. Ibid., p. 555.

13. John Robertson, *The Art and Music of John Lennon* (New York: Carol Publishing Group: New York, 1991).

14. Norman, p. 521.

15. Ibid., p. 548.

16. Ibid., p. 570.

17. Ibid., p. 548.

18. Apple Corps is pronounced "apple core" as a pun.

19. Norman, p. 555.

20. Elizabeth Thomson and David Gutman, *The Lennon Companion: Twenty-Five Years of Comment* (New York: Schirmer Books, 1987), pp. 167–68.

21. Robertson, p. 90.

22. Ibid., p. 92.

23. Ibid., p. 93.

24. Ibid., p. 107.

25. Ibid.

26. Goldman, p. 309.

27. Ibid.

28. Ibid., p. 319.

29. Robertson, p. 97.

30. Norman, p. 575.

31. Goldman, p. 316.

32. Norman, p. 579.

33. Goldman, p. 321.

34. Ibid., p. 326.

35. Ibid., p. 327.

36. Ibid., p. 331.

37. Ibid., p. 332.

38. This is one of the few times McCartney (Mac) would precede Lennon (Len).

39. Goldman, p. 336.

40. ATV music was later purchased by pop sensation Michael Jackson.

41. Giuliano and Giuliano, p. 92.

42. Goldman, p. 344.

43. Elizabeth Partridge, *John Lennon: All I Want Is The Truth* (New York: Viking Press, 2005), p. 2.

44. Goldman, p. 346.
45. Giuliano and Giuliano, p. 98.
46. Ibid., p. 235.
47. Norman, p. 598.
48. Partridge, p. 154.
49. Giuliano and Giuliano, p. 103.
50. Norman, p. 608.

Chapter 7

MOVING ON

As soon as people want peace . . . they will have it.

—*John Lennon, as quoted in* John and Yoko's Year of Peace

When they returned to the United Kingdom, John and Yoko decided to embark on a family vacation, taking Kyoko and Julian to Scotland to visit Mater and Stanley. Yoko insisted that John drive the car, but his driving had not improved over the years. En route to Scotland, John stripped the gearbox in the car, and Les Anthony needed to bring a second car to the family so they could complete their journey.

After spending some time with Mater, John decided to take his family on a day trip to see more of Scotland. John drove toward the Kyle of Tongue, and as he came to a bend in the road, he crashed the car in a ditch. John immediately pulled Julian from the car to make sure he was not injured. Yoko, who was in the backseat with Kyoko, was hurt the worst. She had a back injury and needed 14 stitches on her face. She was under special precautions because she was once again pregnant. John and Kyoko also had stitches, but Julian was fine other than being a little shaken up by the event. Yoko later preserved the car with the blood still visible inside on a pedestal outside the Kenwood living room window to serve as a constant reminder that they needed to be grateful they survived.

Soon after the accident, John returned to the studio to record *Abbey Road* with the Beatles. Yoko insisted on being there in spite of her injuries from the car accident, and so John had a huge bed delivered from Harrod's department store so that she could remain on bed rest. John contributed the song "Come Together," which he intended initially to be about Timothy Leary's failed campaign for California governor, but as the song developed he transformed into a free association about his life with Yoko. Throughout the song he interjected whispers of "shoot me." John also included the song "I Want You (She's So Heavy)" on the album as a love song to Yoko, and the tune "Because." George contributed "Something," a love song he wrote for his wife, Patty Boyd, and "Here Comes the Sun." Paul contributed "Oh! Darling" and "Maxwell's Silver Hammer." Ringo offered "Octopus's Garden." The closing track was called "The End." The album cover was shot on the street in front of the studio as the four strolled across the crosswalk. John took the lead in a white suit, and Ringo followed wearing a suit and tie. Then came Paul in bare feet, and George in denim. It became one of the most famous album covers in the history of rock music.

Abbey Road's release helped to quell speculation among fans that Paul was dead, and it also gave the public a sense that maybe things were not as bad as they suspected among the Beatles. But the publicity photograph for the album conveyed a different message. None of the Beatles were smiling, and the tension between John and Paul in particular was quite palpable. Difficult business situations and John's relationship with Yoko had taken a terrible toll on their friendship and working relationship.

In August John and Yoko moved into Tittenhurst Park, a 74 acre estate just north of London where their first order of business was to quit heroin. From their early days together at Montagu Square, John and Yoko struggled with heroin addiction, something John blamed on "what the Beatles and others were doing to us,"[1] and shortly after moving into their new home they decided to quit heroin cold turkey. Heroin is one of the most addictive drugs to quit, and the withdrawal symptoms are quite painful and difficult to bear both physically and psychologically.

Panic attacks, chills, muscle cramps, vomiting, and other symptoms afflict the addict, and it took great courage for John to attempt to end his addiction in this difficult way. He later wrote about the harrowing experience in the song "Cold Turkey," the first songwriting credit attributed solely to Lennon. Although the song became popular, John's attempts to quit drugs were less successful. He continued to struggle with heroin addiction for the remainder of his life, and he eventually turned to methadone, a controlled drug that reduces the withdrawal symptoms from heroin.

GOING IT ALONE

In September 1969, the city of Toronto hosted a rock festival called the Rock and Roll Revival that featured popular acts of the day, including The Doors, Alice Cooper, and Chicago, along with pioneers of rock music like Chuck Berry, Little Richard, Jerry Lee Lewis, and Bo Didley. Ticket sales were not going well, so promoter John Brower contacted John Lennon by telephone to see if he would perform.[2] John agreed, and he left London the very next day to make it to the concert on time. John called George Harrison and guitarist Eric Clapton to join him, reaching Eric on Saturday morning just before they departed from London.[3]

As John went onstage at the Varsity Stadium without his former bandmates, the audience lit matches. Clapton, bassist Klaus Voorman, percussionist Alan White, and Yoko Ono joined John in the performance, forming what would be called the Plastic Ono Band. The group selected songs that were fairly easy to perform since they had never played together before: "Blue Suede Shoes," "Money," and "Dizzy Miss Lizzy." The set ended with "Give Peace a Chance."

When they finished, John announced that it was Yoko's turn. She commanded the stage for 20 minutes, yodeling, wailing, and howling as John, Eric, and Klaus's guitars produced feedback and Alan White played drum rolls and other sounds from his percussion set. British newspapers reported that the audience booed her off the stage, but John Robertson claimed that the audience merely stood in silence as John explained this was "1980s music, the wave of the future."[4] Apple issued a live album of the event, which included a calendar for *Year*

One A.P. (After Peace). Allen Klein and John convinced producers to cut the Plastic Ono Band's performance from the official film of the festival. Years later, home videos of the event demonstrated the extent to which John remixed the original tapes for the album to remove Yoko's sound effects during his set with the band.[5]

Playing with the Plastic Ono Band allowed John to realize that he could perform successfully on stage without the Beatles. The Plastic Ono Band did not have a defined membership—it consisted of whoever happened to be playing with John and Yoko at the time. The band consisted of John, Yoko, Eric Clapton, Klaus Voormann, and Ringo Starr when they recorded the single "Cold Turkey," which had Yoko's "Don't Worry Kyoko" on the flip side. The single rose to number 14 on the British charts, and to 30 on U.S. charts, not a bad showing given that American radio thought the song was about drug use rather than withdrawal and refused to play it.[6] It was John's second hit without the Beatles in just four months. When John returned to London, he told Allen Klein he was going to leave the Beatles. John made the announcement formally at the next Beatles meeting, and no one seemed to be particularly surprised or concerned, and his decision was not made public at the time.[7]

On October 9, 1969, Yoko miscarried again. It was John's 29th birthday. To recover, they went to Greece where they tried yet again to kick their drug habits. When they returned to London they released *Wedding Album (with Yoko Ono)*, which contained no music. One side consisted of John and Yoko calling out each other's names with sounds of their heartbeats in the background, while the other side included recordings from the Amsterdam bed-in. The album was sold in a white box that included a copy of their wedding certificate and a picture of a slice of wedding cake. The British public largely ignored this album, and it was a no-show on the British charts.

John did not seem to mind that he was distancing himself from the British public, and in November, the wedge only deepened when he returned his Member of the Order of the British Empire (MBE) to the queen. He wrote a short note to the queen and the British prime minister explaining that returning the MBE was in protest against three things: Vietnam; the conflict and death in the African colony Biafra; and "Cold Turkey" losing ground in the charts.[8] This outraged the Brit-

ish public, and some of the people who previously returned their medals in protest of the Beatles' award in 1965, an act that John described
at the time as evidence there "was something wrong with them,"[9] asked
for their status to be reinstated. John later explained that no matter
what he did, the public and the press would notice, so he thought he
should call attention to peace in the process. The reference to "Cold
Turkey" he explained as a gag.[10]

Rather than retreat from the public eye, John began to engage more
actively in controversial and political causes. He pledged his support
to John Hanratty, and with Yoko he pledged to make a film about the
case. Hanratty was accused of murder and hanged in 1962 even though
there were serious doubts about his guilt. John and Yoko adopted the
slogan "Britain murdered Hanratty." While John's rhetoric conveyed
fearlessness, he remained cautious about where he traveled: "I'm scared
of going to Vietnam and Biafra, and until I'm convinced that I'd do
better there than I can do outside of it, I'll stay out . . . don't want to be
a martyr. I'd like to play it safe and be around."[11]

In December 1969, the Plastic Ono Band performed its only European concert as part of a UNICEF benefit in London. Now the band
was called the Plastic Ono Supergroup because they added Keith Moon
of The Who, along with Delaney and Bonnie, a rock band led by a
husband and wife team. The group performed only two songs—"Cold
Turkey" and a version of "Don't Worry Kyoko" that extended more
than 20 minutes into a free form improvisation that pitted Yoko's voice
against brass, electric guitars, feedback, and percussion. As in Toronto,
the audience responded with silence when the performance ended.[12]
This was John's last live performance in England.

On the same day as the UNICEF concert, John and Yoko had billboards installed all over the world in major cities with the message
"War is over, if you want it. Happy Christmas from John and Yoko."
The billboards were vandalized in London.[13] Some people doubted it
would really have any effect, but John explained that Coca-Cola believed their advertisements would sell products, so he should also believe that his poster campaign would make a difference.[14]

In spite of the range of controversy and some measure of indifference about John's creative work, John had a spotlight cast on him at
the end of the year through various public events and accolades. The

BBC created a documentary titled *The World of John and Yoko,* which involved filming the Lennons for five days as they moved from their home to Apple and the recording studio. *Rolling Stone* named John Lennon "Man of the Year." Anthropologist and sociologist Desmond Morris chose John as "Man of the Decade." As the two talked at Tittenhurst, John expressed optimism about the future and the possibility for social change.[15]

John and Yoko returned to Toronto before the year's end to announce the "Music and Peace Conference of the World," a free festival planned for July 1970 that promised performances by the Beatles, the Rolling Stones, Bob Dylan, and Elvis, among others. In one respect, it was an effort to gain some distance from a recent concert in Altamont, California, where just a few weeks earlier the Rolling Stones performed and Hell's Angels reacted violently to the crowd rather than providing security. Scores of fans were beaten and one young man was killed.

While in Canada, John met philosopher Marshall McLuhan and spent 40 minutes with Prime Minister Pierre Trudeau. He and Yoko stayed with Ronnie Hawkins, a rock musician, and his wife at their ranch near Toronto. The Hawkinses graciously allowed John and Yoko to stay in their room, and they hired macrobiotic chefs to prepare food according to the strict diet guidelines Yoko enforced. The celebrity couple's stay was a bit challenging for the Hawkinses: John and Yoko overflowed the bath tub, causing the living room ceiling to collapse, and the phone bill from their week-long stay was $5,000.[16]

The visit to Canada included some snowy weather, giving John some time to complete a series of lithographs while he was there. The lithographs were converted into posters, some of which portrayed images of the couple's honeymoon and drawings of the newlyweds having sex. John autographed each before they were sold to people around the world, and when the posters were later placed on public display in Britain and the United States, several were seized and deemed unacceptable for public view.

The day after Christmas, John and Yoko went to Denmark to negotiate custody arrangements for Kyoko. Tony Cox was remarried and living with Kyoko in a farmhouse in a remote region of the country. John and Yoko ended up staying for three weeks. They cut off their hair and became interested in outer space and cosmic consciousness.

John Brower, who had been arranging the Toronto concert, joined John and Yoko in Denmark. Brower disagreed with John's new ideas for the Toronto show. John wanted the three-day event to be free, but Brower did not. He was afraid to speak up because he knew John had a temper, and he later reflected:

John was filled with a rage that was with him every moment that he lived. When he really let it out, he was mercilessly scathing. I tell you, you did not want to be on the other end of that barrage. I never saw anyone stand up to him. Never![17]

Plans for the event finally collapsed amid a range of accusations from all involved, including claims that John and Yoko were naïve.[18] John wrote a 2,500-word explanation that appeared in *Rolling Stone* magazine in April called "Have We All Forgotten What Vibes Are?"

INSTANT KARMA, PRIMAL SCREAMS

When Lennon returned to London in early January, he wrote the song "Instant Karma" using the same three-chord sequence from "All You Need Is Love." He invited George Harrison, Klaus Voorman, and drummer Alan White to the Abbey Road studio. Phil Spector joined them to produce the single, and John was so impressed with his work that he continued to work with Spector for the next two years. Many believed Spector was the greatest producer ever. He created what came to be known as the Wall of Sound, which combined rhythm vocals, horns, echoes, and other electronic effects.[19]

Five days after the single was released, John appeared on BBC TVs *Top of the Pops* show to perform the song "Instant Karma." With newly shorn hair and an armband attached to his faded denim jacket that read "People for Peace," John played piano over a backing tape accompanied on the stage by Alan White and Klaus Voorman. Yoko sat blindfolded in a chair displaying signs that read "Smile," "Peace," and "Hope." She had a microphone and occasionally leaned in to it, but no sounds could be heard over the band. Young people danced in the background around the stage, seeming to enjoy the song, which soon went to number five on the British charts and number three on the

America charts. It was the first solo-Beatle single to sell a million cop-ies in the United States.

In February 1970, John had what biographer Albert Goldman de-scribed as a quiet nervous breakdown. He went to bed and refused to see anyone. Goldman claimed that John had multiple personalities that stemmed from childhood trauma and that at times he dissociated himself from reality, entering a dreamlike state. His claims are based in part on John's statements about this experience:

> If I am on my own for three days, doing nothing, I almost leave myself completely . . . I'm up there watching myself . . . I can see my hands and realize they're moving, but it's a robot that's doing it . . . It's frightening really.[20]

Goldman also claimed that John's break from the Beatles was psychic suicide.[21] John needed to be busy, to have goals he was working to achieve, and to be with people who understood him. Although the Beatles created conflicts for John, they were a known and safe place for him. Without them, he faced much uncertainty.

Finally, on March 5, 1970, John and Yoko checked into the London Clinic hoping to clean up and rid themselves of drug addictions once and for all. John told a startled reporter that Yoko was a junkie, and at the time they were both struggling with heroin addiction and metha-done.[22] When they returned to Tittenhurst at the end of the month, the press announced that Yoko was again pregnant.

Soon after, Paul publicly announced that he was leaving the Beatles. John lashed back by saying that Paul couldn't quit since John had al-ready fired him. Paul blamed Yoko for the breakup, and the press picked up on this. In fact it was John who initiated the breakup, but Allen Klein and Paul convinced him to keep it quiet until *Abbey Road* met with some success. John later recalled that he was the one who started the band, and he was also the one who ended it.[23]

As the Beatles breakup began to sink in, John received a copy of the book *The Primal Scream: Primal Therapy, the Cure for Neurosis* in the mail. He became intrigued with the ideas and sought out the book's author, Los Angeles psychiatrist Arthur Janov. Janov believed that tak-ing a person back to early childhood and making him scream the pain he experienced when his wants were not fulfilled would alleviate all of the problems that had resulted from those unfulfilled needs, so the person could begin life again. At John and Yoko's request, Janov traveled to Tittenhurst with his wife, Vivien. He treated John and Yoko daily through April, offering advice that included encouraging John to visit Julian (which caused Yoko to threaten suicide because she was afraid John would reunite with Cynthia).[24] Janov was surprised at the extent of John's pain and the fact that "at the center of all that fame and wealth and adulation was just a lonely little kid."[25]

Paul planned to release a solo album called *McCartney* on April 17, the Beatles album *Let It Be* was scheduled for release April 20, and Ringo's solo album *Sentimental Journal* was also set to be released at this time. Paul proceeded with his plans, even though it jeopardized publicity for the Beatles album.

John asked Phil Spector to work on the sound tracks for *Let It Be*. The tapes had been sitting idle for about six months, and something needed to be done with them. Spector added his Wall of Sound, reportedly without Paul's involvement. The album would be the Beatles' 12th and final studio album, even though the songs were recorded before the *Abbey Road* album. It included John's 1967 song "Across the Universe," which sat in the vault for nearly two years after its initial recording because it was not appropriate for release as a single. John began the song years earlier when he was still married to Cynthia, waking up from a dream to write the opening lyrics on paper. George Martin first contributed the piece to a World Wildlife Fund Charity Album after adding some bird sounds in the opening, and then they included it on the *Let It Be* album. John later complained that the recording was not particularly good because "the guitars are out of tune and I'm singing out of tune because I'm psychologically destroyed and no one is supporting me or helping me with it, and the song was never done properly."[26] In spite of John's dissatisfaction with the song, the album went to number one in Britain and the United States, remaining on the charts for more than a year. *Let It Be* later won an Academy Award for Best Film Score and a Grammy for best original music sound track.

In May, John and Yoko went to Los Angeles to continue primal therapy treatments. Janov asked the couple to plan to spend between four and six months in therapy. They attended the center daily as Janov continued private sessions. John and Yoko joined group sessions three times each week, but they had to return to London in July because John's visa expired. Janov thought the sessions were ending abruptly and perhaps too soon. He hoped to work for another year with John to help him through his anger and pain.[27] But Yoko discredited Janov to John, and she began to conduct primal therapy sessions with him. In late August, Yoko miscarried again.

In late September, John heard from his father after more than a year of little to no communication.[28] His father's young wife had given birth to a son they named David, whose presence did not particularly interest John, and Alf was about to begin writing his own autobiography. John invited Alf and his family to Tittenhurst to celebrate his 30th birthday. When Alf arrived, both he and his wife were taken aback by John's appearance. He now had a beard and appeared pale and haggard. John, no doubt fueled by his recent experiences with primal therapy, unleashed a rage of fury against his father. Alf was frightened for his life. Soon after, John repossessed Alf's home in Brighton.

By September, John was working on a solo album with Klaus Voorman on bass guitar, Ringo Starr on drums, and Billy Preston on keyboards. Yoko recorded her own album at the same time with the same group of musicians, planning a release that would occur simultaneously with John's. The first song on John's album, "Mother," went to the root of his deepest pain: "Mother, you had me, I never had you . . . Father, you left me, I never left you." Another autobiographical song that vented some of John's pent-up anger at his childhood was "Working Class Hero," directed against Aunt Mimi and his childhood at Mendips. The song was written as a folk tune and John spoke the words in rhythm. The tune begins, "As soon as you're born, they make you feel small."

The *Plastic Ono Band* album, with John Lennon and the Plastic Ono Band, was released in December. It reflects John's rage and his feelings that all his problems could be traced to his childhood trauma. The album is very symmetrical, oscillating between fear and rage, past and present. The song "God" included the line "I was the walrus, but now I'm John." The final song "My Mummy's Dead" has only one verse and set to the melody of the children's song "Three Blind Mice." Some critics called it his most radical musical statement.[29]

Around the time of the album's release, John went to New York and gave an extended interview with *Rolling Stone* writer Jann Wenner. John and Yoko had spent time with Wenner in San Francisco earlier in the year when they were undergoing therapy. The interview was so extensive it was published in two issues of the magazine. The interview was a tell-all account of Lennon's time with the Beatles, whom he sometimes referred to as the Beastles. He went on record admitting that Brian Epstein was gay, but denied that the two had ever had an affair. He described the mayhem, the need to comply with wishes of dignitaries, how advisers attempted to limit their comments on important issues of the day, and he exposed the realities of touring, including the drug use. John claimed the boys resented performing for idiots. John dismissed George's first solo album and its wildly popular single "My Sweet Lord," and he called Paul's recent album *McCartney* rubbish, claiming that Paul and Linda simply imitated John. He explained:

> If I could be a f***in' fisherman, I would . . . If I had the capabilities of being something other than I am, I would. It's no fun being an artist . . . and those f***in' bastards [the public], they're just sucking us to death . . . I'd rather be in the audience really, but I'm not capable of it. . . . But the pain . . . if you don't know, man, there's no pain.[30]

John dismissed the 1960s, claiming that nothing was accomplished in that time.

The year 1970 was not completely devoted to John's personal search for inner peace. In part because of the British public's racist attitudes toward Yoko, John became more interested in social equity and overcoming racism. At the time Britain was struggling with its complicated relationship with South Africa, and the Black Power movement that began in the United States had spread to England. John paid the fines for a group of antiapartheid protestors who disrupted a Scottish-South African rugby match, an act that Britain's Black Power movement leader Michael X noticed. Michael X approached John and Yoko for funds to support the Black House, a home for delinquent teens in North London, and he played on John's guilt by claiming that the Beatles stole the black people's rhythms.[31] John agreed to help fund a soup kitchen at the Black House, and he and Yoko donated their shorn locks from their haircuts in Denmark earlier in the year.

While they were in New York, John and Yoko filmed *Up Your Legs Forever*, a 75-minute film of leg shots of 300 people. At the end of the film, the camera swung up to expose John and Yoko's bare buttocks, followed by John reading the credits. They followed this with the film *Fly*, which recorded a black fly walking on the body of a naked female actress. John was coproducer and contributed background music to the film.

When they finished filming in New York, the couple went to Tokyo to visit Yoko's family. It was John's first time in Japan, and his first acquaintance with Yoko's parents, Eisuke and Isoko Ono. Eisuke was president of a bank in Japan, and the family enjoyed great wealth and prestige in Tokyo. After the *Two Virgins* album, the family issued a public statement claiming they were not proud of Yoko.[32] In spite of any reservations the Ono family may have had, John seemed to get along well with Yoko's family, even though Yoko's father told his daughter that her first husband was better looking.[33]

STRUGGLING ON

John recorded "Power to the People" in January 1970. It was his attempt to reflect the interests of his new friendships among the British Trotskyist movement as he shifted his interests from his own self-examination that dominated the 1970s outward to the masses.[34] Phil Spector produced the song as a single, which soon climbed to number 7 in the U.K. and number 11 in the U.S. charts.

Although the Beatles were no longer recording as a group, their financial and business problems were far from resolved. Paul had long been distrustful of Allen Klein and wanted to dismiss him in spite of the money Klein brought to the band.[35] Paul wanted the Eastmans to manage them, and he tied up the band's money in a lawsuit. Paul finally levied a lawsuit against Klein and the other three Beatles to legally sever their relationship. Paul was the only one of the band to actually appear in court. The hearing, at which Judge Justice Stamp presided, lasted eleven days.

John and Yoko continued to live at Tittenhurst, and the seven-year-old Julian visited them at the estate. Yoko's daughter Kyoko, however, was not a frequent visitor. Her father was doubtful that John and Yoko's lifestyle was best for the child, and he remained deeply upset about the car accident in Scotland. Further, Tony did not want Kyoko subjected to the constant media attention that surrounded her mother and John. In mid-April, Tony left London with Kyoko and his girlfriend, Melinda, leaving no clues about his whereabouts or plans.[36]

Finally one of Tony's friends let it slip that he was in Majorca completing a course on transcendental meditation.[37] John and Yoko flew to the Spanish island and attempted to kidnap Kyoko from Tony Cox. They were detained by police for four hours after they took Kyoko from a children's camp. John confessed to kidnapping the child and then was arrested. Both John and Yoko's passports were confiscated, and they had to stay in Spain until the case was resolved. Allen Klein found a lawyer who altered John's original confession, and John and Yoko were not punished.

When John and Yoko returned to Tittenhurst, they began to work on the album *Imagine*. The album was recorded in a week at John's home studio, and when it was finished, John and Yoko flew to the United States for Phil Spector to work on the production. The title song for the album, "Imagine," conveyed John's idea that the world is really just one group of people as he offered a plea for world peace. John's ideas for the song came from Yoko's book *Grapefruit*, and years later he admitted that he should have given her co-credit for writing the song.[38] The lyrics to the song stand in stark contrast to his earlier yet ambiguous call for more violent action in "Revolution," and the two songs placed side-by-side help to show the contradictions in John's politics. On the one hand he seemed to call for violence to change society, while on the other he encouraged people to dream of nonviolent change. Some considered the song to be a "rich celebrity's soft-minded Utopia," and a more cynical fan asked *Rolling Stone* to "Imagine John Lennon with no possessions,[39]" but it remains one of his most famous songs.

Another song on the *Imagine* album, "How Do You Sleep," had immediate attention among fans interested in the now public feud between Paul and John. It exposed John's feelings that Paul was dishonest, lacked talent, and was a hypocrite. By contrast, the album also contained the song "Jealous Guy," which offered an apology of sorts to Yoko and exposed John's growing interest in feminism.[40] The song,

"Gimme Some Truth," is a protest song that included a dig at U.S. President Richard Nixon, whom Lennon referred to as "Tricky Dicky."

The title track "Imagine" was made into the first full-length rock documentary video. Filmed at Tittenhurst, the documentary begins with John and Yoko walking through the fog and to the front door of their home. John played the song "Imagine" at a white piano in a large room while Yoko opens the shutters on the windows, one by one, making the room brighter as the song progresses.

Other scenes in the documentary give a glimpse of John's life at the time, which continued to create fanatical interest among some of his fans. One young man captured in the video believed that if John looked in his eyes he would be healed. The young man wrote to John from a mental hospital, and when he was released, he remained outside the gate at Tittenhurst. John was troubled by this and did not want to meet the young man, but when others insisted, John went to the gate. The camera crew captured the young man walking toward John, looking in his eyes, and then without a word, he turned and walked slowly away.[41]

As their work on *Imagine* concluded, Yoko convinced John they should move to New York City. They visited the city early in the summer. On June 3, 1971, John took his first walk on the streets of New York. When he was in the city with the Beatles, he did not have this kind of freedom, but now he could roam the streets and night clubs, meeting other celebrities like Andy Warhol and Frank Zappa.

George Harrison visited John when he was in New York, and the two worked on some songs together. George was planning the Concert for Bangladesh at Madison Square Garden in New York City on August 1 with Ravi Shankar. In 1971 East Pakistan was struggling to become an independent state (Bangladesh), and the war and political turmoil resulted in an enormous refugee problem in India that was further complicated by a cyclone that brought devastating floods. The concert was one way to bring public attention to the humanitarian crisis and to raise money to help alleviate some of the terrible conditions people faced.

The concert lineup included Bob Dylan, Eric Clapton, Billy Preston, and others, and it raised $250,000 in ticket sales alone for Bangladesh's refugees. Harrison wanted the Beatles to reunite for the event, performing live for the first time in five years. Ringo agreed immediately. Paul at first agreed, but then declined. John also agreed at first, but George was very clear that Yoko was not to join them and she would not have a slot in the lineup as a solo artist. John wanted to be in the concert, and when he told Yoko so, they had a terrible argument. John became so angry during the argument, he smashed his wire-rimmed glasses in his clenched fist, then left for the airport and a return flight to London.[42] He never performed at the concert.

NOTES

1. Philip Norman, *John Lennon: The Life* (New York: Harper Collins Publishers, 2008), p. 617.

2. John Robertson, *The Art and Music of John Lennon* (New York: Carol Publishing Group, 1991), p. 116.

3. Geoffrey Giuliano and Brenda Giuliano, *The Lost Lennon Interviews* (Holbrook, MA: Adams Media Corporation, 1996), p. 78.

4. Robertson, p. 117.

5. Ibid., p. 118.

6. Norman, p. 626.

7. Albert Goldman, *The Lives of John Lennon* (New York: William Morrow and Company, 1988), p. 359.

8. Norman, p. 628.

9. Giuliano and Giuliano, p. 4.

10. Ibid., p. 82.

11. Ibid., p. 86.

12. Robertson, p. 120.

13. Ibid., p. 121.

14. Giuliano and Giuliano, p. 83.

15. Norman, p. 630.

16. Goldman, p. 364.

17. Ibid., p. 368.

18. Richardson, p. 121.

19. This Wall of Sound was different than the massive speaker system, also called the Wall of Sound, used by the Grateful Dead at concert venues.

20. Goldman, p. 374.

21. Ibid., p. 375.

22. Norman, p. 637.

23. Ibid., p. 624.

24. Goldman, p. 384.

25. Norman, p. 640.

26. Robertson, pp. 80–81.

27. Norman, pp. 648–49.

28. Ibid., p. 652.

29. Robertson, p. 127.

30. Jann Wenner, *Lennon Remembers* (San Francisco, CA: Straight Arrow Books, 1971), p. 106.

31. Norman, p. 636.

32. Ibid., p. 660.

33. Ibid., p. 661.

34. Robertson, p. 132.

35. Goldman, p. 394.

36. Norman, pp. 666–67.

37. Ibid.

38. Robertson, p. 139.

39. Thomson and Gutman, p. 12.

40. Robertson, p. 137.

41. May Pang and Henry Edwards, *Loving John* (New York: Warner Bros, 1983), p. 39.

42. Ibid., p. 46.

Chapter 8

SEARCHING FOR PEACE IN NEW YORK CITY

In August of 1971, John left Britain for the last time. He and Yoko moved into the St. Regis Hotel on Fifth Avenue in New York City. Feeling misunderstood in England and weary of the disdain the British public showed toward Yoko,[1] the two looked to New York City for more understanding and acceptance of them and their art, and they planned to become leaders of the New York avant-garde. The couple quickly settled into two suites on the 17th floor where they stored their items, set up offices, and established an improvised recording studio and work space for their ongoing film and album projects. John told reporters: "If I'd lived in ancient times, I'd have lived in Rome . . . Today America is the Roman Empire and New York is Rome itself."[2]

A young woman named May Pang first met John and Yoko when she was hired as a secretary at ABKCO Music and Records, an independent record label, music publisher, and film and video production company based in New York City. Not long after their first meeting, May started working for John and Yoko full-time as a personal assistant. Some of the hotel suites the couple occupied were turned into offices for Joko Productions, a film company John and Yoko established with plans to create one film per week. Their first film attempt after settling into New York was called *Clock*. The background consisted of Yoko making phone calls and John playing 1950s rock songs on his acoustic guitar. They also had a photo studio and a seamstress set up in their suites. One of their first projects was a concept art show with flies, which coincided with an album Yoko released called *Fly*. John wanted the public to realize the artists like Yoko were visionaries, not groups like the Beatles.[3]

On October 9, 1971, John's 31st birthday, Yoko's one-woman show "This Is Not Here" opened at the Everson Museum of Fine Arts in Syracuse, New York. The name for the exhibit was also the slogan posted over the door at the Tittenhurst estate. She had 50,000 square feet to fill in the museum, and she created one of the most elaborate and costly exhibits housed outside a major art center, supported in large part by John's generous contribution.[4] Their film *Clock* played continually in the foyer as visitors entered to view the exhibits. One gallery was filled with "Part Paintings" of objects that ranged from clouds to images of the Ku Klux Klan. Another exhibit included Yoko's past work, such as the "Eternal Clock." Yet another exhibit was the "Water Event," which included John's work "Napoleon's Bladder" (a pink mass inside a clear plastic bag), a milk bottle from George Harrison, and a green plastic garbage bag from Ringo with a message about a sea sponge that was caught off the Libyan coast taped to the outside. Yoko sent rumors that the Beatles might reunite at the museum, and fans converged on the museum. On the first day, 8,000 young people showed up hoping to see John. They trashed the exhibition, and water went everywhere. Finally the poet Allen Ginsberg was able to calm the crowd by using a chant.

After the opening night, John and Yoko celebrated with Phil Spector, Klaus Voorman, Ringo and Maureen Starkey, and Allen Ginsberg. John played guitar as guests sang along to "He's Got the Whole World in His Hands" and "Attica State," one of John's new songs that served as a protest to killings at a New York State jail. Upside down plastic trashcans served as impromptu drums as party guests joined in song. John's cake had a guitar on it with the words "Happy birthday John from Yoko and the whole world."

In November, John and Yoko moved to a basement apartment on Bank Street in New York City's West End. The apartment consisted of small two main rooms—a living room and a slightly larger bedroom—along with a tiny kitchen. The West End teemed with writers, artists, poets, and political activists, and John and Yoko thrived in this environment, where they connected with Bob Dylan and the activists Jerry Rubin and Abbie Hoffman. John made new friends, including songwriter and street musician David Peel, photographer Bob Gruen and political activist Jon Hendricks. Their apartment became a salon as friends frequently stopped in to discuss issues and concerns of the day. John spoke out regularly against racism, sexism, the Vietnam War, and other injustices he witnessed.

John and Yoko quickly became part of the larger political activist scene. One of the first things they did was attend a December 10 rally at the Crisler Arena in Ann Arbor, Michigan, on behalf of poet and activist John Sinclair called "Ten for Two." Sinclair was sentenced to 10 years in prison after giving an undercover police officer two marijuana cigarettes, outraging activists and members of the counterculture movement across the country. Joko filmed the rally as 15,000 people looked on from the audience, eagerly anticipating the possible reunion of the Beatles. This was John's first public performance in the United States since the Beatles last show. John and Yoko went on stage at 3 AM and played four songs that were unfamiliar to the crowd. Leslie Bacon and David Peel backed up on guitar, and Jerry Rubin sat in on percussion. The event was not one of John's best: his acoustic guitar was difficult for the audience to hear and the strap broke, Yoko was out of step with the rest of the group, and the audience seemed disappointed. John ended his performance by asking for Sinclair's release and then he promptly left the stage. He was clearly not concerned about pleasing the audience. Much to everyone's surprise, however, Sinclair was released a few days later while appealing his conviction.

A week after the Sinclair rally, there was a day of protest in New York City against the Attica state prison riot, in which 28 prisoners had been killed and 9 people had been taken hostage. The Apollo Theater in Harlem hosted a concert to benefit relatives of the victims who were both prisoners and guards. The show primarily consisted of soul musicians, but John and Yoko gave a brief surprise performance.

The next day the couple flew to Houston, Texas, to attend court hearings concerning custody rights of Kyoko. Tony Cox was now living in Houston, his new wife Melinda's hometown. When Cox ignored court orders concerning Kyoko's custody, he was charged with contempt of court and put in jail for five days.[5] The judge ordered that Kyoko should be returned to her mother, but when Cox was released from jail on bail, he and Melinda took the child and disappeared again.

THE PUBLIC AND THE FBI

The new year was a politically charged one. President Richard Nixon was running for re-election. The voting age was lowered to 18, which meant that 12 million new voters could go to the polls. Politicians and media pundits were uncertain what this could mean, and some speculated that public figures and activists like John Lennon could have some influence on how young people would cast their vote.

In early 1972, John and Yoko did a series of talk show events. In January they appeared on *The David Frost Show*, where they performed "John Sinclair," "It's So Hard," "Attica State," and "Luck of the Irish" with Elephant's Memory, a New York bar band, as their backup. These songs would be on John's next album, *Some Time in New York City*. The songs were not without controversy. When John performed his new protest song "Attica State," a couple yelled at him from the audience, accusing him of glorifying criminals, but other members of the audience came to John's defense. John and Yoko also appeared later in the year on *The Mike Douglas Show* and *The Dick Cavett Show*, performing music and espousing their political views.

John's new album, *Some Time in New York City*, was released in March. The songs reflected influences of his new home along with his more active political engagement: "New York City" conveyed John's sense of liberation from England, while "Woman Is the Nigger of the World" shared his newfound feminism. In addition to his political protests about Attica State and John Sinclair's imprisonment, John included a song, "Sunday Bloody Sunday," which conveyed his anger over the violence in Ireland and his further dissociation from his home in England:

Keep Ireland for the Irish
Put the English back to sea!

John seemed to become increasingly infatuated with revolutionary violence during this time.[6] He marched in a street protest on behalf of the

Irish Revolutionary Army just a week after Bloody Sunday, when soldiers had shot and killed 13 civilians in Derry, Northern Ireland. John became friends with A. J. Webberman of the Rock Liberation Front, which was dedicated to saving rock music from commercialism. Lennon assigned royalties from his song "Luck of the Irish" to the Northern Irish Aid (the IRA in New York).

John's political activism did not go unnoticed by the U.S. government. The Federal Bureau of Investigation (FBI), which serves both as a federal criminal investigative body and an internal intelligence agency, began paying attention to John when his album *Unfinished Music No. 1: Two Virgins (with Yoko Ono)* was released. John was under surveillance when he visited the West Coast for primal therapy sessions, although he was likely unaware of this at the time. When he moved to New York and participated in the Sinclair rally, one of many FBI agents at the event determined that John was "a strong believer in the [Yippie][7] movement and in the overthrow of the present society in America today."[8]

Certain members of the government went after Lennon because they feared his plans would result in money pouring into the New Left. Conservative Senator Strom Thurmond wrote to Attorney General John Mitchell on February 3, 1972, outlining what he thought were John's plans to combine a rock concert tour with antiwar activities in order to influence the youth vote. Mitchell quickly contacted the U.S. Immigration and Naturalization Services (INS). G. Gordon Liddy, a member of the Committee to Re-Elect the President (CREEP) believed John and people like him (including students and activists) were enemies of the United States, and he supported Mitchell and Thurmond's concerns about John. Shortly after this, the INS informed John and Yoko that their visas were recalled and they would need to leave the country by March 15.

John and Yoko hired lawyer Leon Wildes to appeal their case. Wildes was then president of the American Immigration Lawyers Association, and he had more than 15 years experience with immigration and naturalization legal cases.[9] Wildes seemed doubtful there was much chance for the Lennons to win, even though he thought it was clear they were being punished for their political views. Wildes thought their only hope was to take the case to federal court. John's former drug conviction in

London presented a challenge in the legal aspects of his case, but the UK law had since been amended, and prosecutors had to prove that defendants knowingly possessed the illegal substance. John claimed he did not know the marijuana was in the Montagu Square flat, and he believed it was probably left behind by former resident Jimi Hendrix or planted by police.[10]

In spring of 1972, John turned from political activism to focus more on his INS case and Kyoko. In March, the Houston court upheld the ruling that Yoko should have sole custody of her daughter and that Kyoko should be raised in the United States. But Tony, Melinda, and Kyoko were still nowhere to be found, and so little changed for John and Yoko. John used the case to plead for mercy from the INS court, claiming that the family should not be torn apart if Yoko were permitted to stay in the United States and John was forced to leave. By this time the FBI suspected that the Lennons were conspiring with the Coxes to hide the child to help with the antideportation case. These suspicions were never proven.

In April, John and Yoko attended a National Peace Rally in New York's Duffy Square, where they led the crowd in singing "Give Peace a Chance," but their political activities had scaled back considerably. John was now well aware that the federal government had an interest in him. He had good reason to believe the telephone at their Bank Street apartment had been bugged, and undercover FBI agents had been assigned to follow John, Yoko, and their employees, including photographer Bob Gruen. Friend Dan Richter later explained, "I was expecting [John] to be put in a bag at any moment and hauled off to the airport—or even to be assassinated . . . It was scary."[11] Yet this surveillance did not significantly change John's daily routines or habits. As he continued to record music and move about New York City, he consumed alcohol and partook of other substances just as he had done in the past. Gruen later remarked, "The cops could have come along and busted John any time they wanted. It wasn't like we were sneaking around. We were drinking and driving and smoking."[12]

The FBI and the federal government did not anticipate the mass public support John enjoyed. As news of his INS case spread, the *New York Times* ran an editorial supporting him, friend Jon Hendricks secured tens of thousands of signatures on a petition supporting John, the head of the national auto workers union publicly supported him, and New York's mayor, John Lindsay, appealed to the commissioner of the INS for John's deportation case to be rescinded.[13]

By June, John's album *Some Time in New York City* was largely considered to be a failure. It only reached 48 on American charts and 11 in England. John gave Yoko credit for four songs on the album she cowrote, and her publishing company, Ono Music, claimed half the copyright on these songs. Northern Music promptly filed a $1 million lawsuit against John, claiming that he violated the 1965 agreement that gave the company full rights to any song he wrote. John countersued for $9 million in what he claimed were unpaid foreign royalties.[14]

None of this reflected well on John's public image, and so in August, with Leon Wildes's encouragement, John agreed to perform a benefit concert initiated by reporter Geraldo Rivera. Called One to One, the proceeds from the concert benefited special needs children at the Willowbrook Hospital in New York. John and Yoko performed an afternoon and evening show live at Madison Square Garden with the band Elephant's Memory playing backup. It was later released as *Live in New York City*. John donned a militant-looking army jacket and tinted round eyeglasses as he gave riveting performances of "Mother," "Hound Dog," "Cold Turkey," and "Come Together." Allen Klein understood that the public did not want to see John perform with Yoko, but John did not change his plans to have her by his side on the stage. Klein had to give away 5,000 free tickets just to fill the house. In the end, however, the shows raised $180,000 in ticket revenue and another $350,000 in rights for ABC television to air the show.[15] The concerts would mark Klein's last professional work with Lennon. When his contract expired in March, he was fired as manager.

Once Klein was out of the picture, Harold Seider assumed responsibility for the John's business matters. He hired lawyers and accountants, and made John sign checks so that he was aware of what he was spending, something John had never done before. Seider attempted to make John financially responsible and to get his spending to a reasonable amount, roughly $300,000 per year. Also, he quickly eliminated financially bad business ventures like Joko Productions and Apple. Seider wanted John to be able to live comfortably without needing to produce anything.[16] Seider had formerly worked as Klein's legal counsel,

John Lennon performs at New York's Madison Square Garden on August 30, 1972. (AP Photo/ File.)

and when John hired him, he was also vice president of United Artists Record Management. He was granted special permission to work for John on a part-time basis, but needed to be careful because of potential conflicts of interest.

On November 7, 1972, Richard Nixon was reelected president of the United States. John and Yoko were at the studio working on her solo album *Approximately Infinite Universe* when they heard the news. John was sure Nixon would want him deported, and be began to become quite drunk. The couple went to Jerry Rubin's apartment later that evening to commiserate about the election. John disappeared for a time into a bedroom with another woman, and it was clear to everyone what was happening behind the closed door. Yoko was quite hurt by his actions. Later that evening, John became hostile, screaming and threatening violence. He shouted out, "I'm going to join the Weathermen! I'm going to shoot a policeman!"[17] He left Rubin's place and returned to his home where he stayed in his bedroom for six months.

At the end of the year, the Lennons moved into the Dakota apartment building on Central Park West in New York City. The building was constructed in the 1880s, and it was named Dakota because at the time it was built, the area was largely undeveloped and the building was considered to be as far away from the city as North or South Dakota. The building is known for its high gables, dormers, balconies, and balustrades, and it was once the film site for Roman Polanski's movie *Rosemary's Baby*. John and Yoko moved into apartment 72 on the seventh floor, where they enjoyed a spacious home with four bedrooms and stunning views of Central Park.

ELUSIVE PEACE

The Lennons remained largely out of the public eye in early 1973. John was not writing music, but Yoko was, and their relationship had become quite strained. John wrote letters and made regular phone calls to Aunt Mimi, but he did not let her know about his unhappiness. When Mimi picked up the telephone, he would answer her "hello" with "It's Himself."[18] The phone calls and letters were newsy, as John shared information about his daily life and reminiscences about Liverpool. Mimi believed he missed his home in England. He invited her to New York, but she replied by telling him, "I'm not going to a land where there's guns, John."[19]

In March, the last troops were withdrawn from Vietnam. The war dead included 3,800,000 Vietnamese, 800,000 Cambodians, 58,178 Americans, and 50,000 Laotians. Since there was no longer a national protest movement against the war, FBI surveillance of John waned, although the deportation case with the INS continued. Yet there was a more hopeful spirit in the air, and on April 1, 1973 (April Fool's Day), John and Yoko held a press conference to announce the founding of Nutopia—a country of peace, without laws, passports, or boundaries. A white handkerchief served as the flag. The coupled explained their wish to have the United Nations recognize them and grant asylum since they were now self-declared residents of this new conceptual land.

After nearly a year of little to no writing, John began to come up with some new songs to meet his record contract obligations, not unlike the way in which he and Paul completed music to fulfill obligations in his Beatles days.[20] He began writing autobiographical songs that reflected the uncertainties he felt in his relationship with Yoko. John began to record this music as the album *Mind Games* in August at the Record Plant East in New York City. The title song was based in part on a book of the same name by Robert Masters and Jean Houston that supported consciousness raising to find fulfillment. The album continued to reveal John and his life through song, including the love song to Yoko called "You Are Here."

Problems between John and Yoko became increasingly pronounced during this time. They argued and withdrew from one another. Yoko seemed to be interested in guitar player David Spinozza, who she hired to help with her latest record project.[21] One evening, knowing that a separation was imminent, Yoko encouraged her assistant May Pang to become involved with John. She told the 22-year-old Pang, "I'd rather see him going out with you. It will make him happy. It will be great. He'll be happy. It's cool. . . . Don't worry about a thing. I'll take care of everything."[22] May was uncertain about what to do. She did not want to lose her job, and she understood how determined Yoko could be. May knew enough about Japanese culture to understand that Japanese women often arranged for mistresses for their husbands, but she still was not comfortable with this. Shortly after Yoko left the room, May began to cry. The next evening, her romantic affair with John Lennon began.

LOST WEEKEND

In September 1973, John and May went to Los Angeles with Harold Seider as John continued to work on the album *Mind Games*. Elliot Mintz met them in the airport, and he served as a type of public relations expert and personal assistant to John during his time in Los Angeles. Once he settled in the city, John reconnected with former Beatles' roadie Mal Evans, who was now living in Los Angeles, and Ringo Starr became a frequent visitor. Former Rolling Stones manager Andrew Loog Oldham loaned John and May record producer Lou Adler's Bel Air home. John was financially broke. Although he was earning money, it went directly to Apple, where it was tied up in a legal dispute. When he arrived in Los Angeles, he secured a $10,000 loan, something he was loathe to do since he did not believe in borrowing money.[23]

John's legal problems continued, even though he was on a different coast. This time he faced a lawsuit for plagiarizing the song "Come Together." The piece opens with a line that is quite similar musically and lyrically to Chuck Berry's song "You Can't Catch Me," where Berry sang "Here come a flattop." John settled out of court, agreeing to record and pay royalties on three songs owned by Morris Levy, who held the copyright for the Chuck Berry song. Rather than record three singles, however, John decided to make an album with the songs Levy accumulated, songs John loved when he was growing up. He turned to Phil Spector, who was living in Los Angeles at the time, and Spector agreed to produce provided he had total control over the album.[24] The recording sessions were referred to as the "Spector Sessions." Celebrities like Jack Nicholson, Warren Beatty, Cher, Mick Jagger, and Joni Mitchell showed up at the recording studio to hear the sessions and join in the party.[25] John and Phil frequently argued during recording sessions, partied, and once were kicked out of a studio when Phil shot a pistol, lodging a bullet in the ceiling.[26] After the gun shot, John told Phil, "Listen, Phil, if you're gonna kill me, kill me. But don't f*** with me ears. I need 'em."[27] In the end, John decided the recordings were not good enough to release, and several years later when they were finally available to the public he had to overdub the vocals.

Yoko kept in close contact with John and May while they were in Los Angeles, and Yoko was clearly in charge of their relationship even though she was in New York.[28] She made multiple phone calls to the couple every day. Once May counted 23 calls in a single day, and the long distance phone bill for one month was as much a $3,000.[29] It was a tangled game they played with one another, but Yoko clearly had considerable power over John.[30]

When the Specter Sessions ended and Phil disappeared after crashing two cars, John began spending his time in nightclubs like the Troubadour and the Rainbow with Ringo Starr, Keith Moon, Harry Nilsson, and others. John drank heavily during this time. Alcohol brought out a dark side in John, and he often became quite violent and angry.[31] On one occasion, his rage resulted in significant damage to Lou Adler's home: broken furniture, a broken chandelier, and damage to the platinum albums that hung on Adler's walls, including Carole King's *Tapestry*. On another occasion, John suspected May was flirting with David

Cassidy, who was enjoying fame as the star of *The Partridge Family* television show. His angry tirade frightened May, but she was afraid to leave him alone. The two returned to New York City the next day, and John went back to the Dakota for one night. The next day, he asked May to travel back to California with him.

Seeking some stability for John and some connection to family, May encouraged him to reunite with Julian, an idea Yoko originally suggested to her. John invited the boy, now 11 years old, to Los Angeles. He had not seen him in two years. Cynthia accompanied Julian as he traveled to Los Angeles to see his father. Yoko was anxious because she did not want John to leave her for Cynthia, and she called John on the telephone incessantly. She tried to make him feel guilty because he could see his son but she was not able to see her daughter, Kyoko.

John and May took Julian to Disneyland, and Cynthia joined them so that Julian would be more comfortable. They had a relaxed time together, and Cynthia and John sometimes reminisced about the old days, including their time with the Maharishi. Cynthia mentioned that she always hoped to have another child with John, but John told her that he was unable to have more children because of the effects of his drug use.[32] Later when a radio interviewer asked John if there was anything in his life he would change if he could, he first replied nothing, but then added that he would have been different with his son Julian.[33] He realized that he did not spend enough time with the boy.

After Cynthia and Julian departed for England, May and John briefly returned to New York as John worked to settle legal matters with Allen Klein and the dissolution of Apple Corps. It was a complicated case because the Beatles' homes and expenses were tied up in the company, including approximately $2 million that John and Yoko charged to Apple Corps.[34] The other Beatles did not want to pay these expenses, nor did they wish to pay for the production of Yoko's albums. When one of the Beatles made a solo album, the money went to Apple and the royalties were frozen. There were many points to negotiate. In the midst of ongoing talks with lawyers, John learned from one member of the legal counsel that Yoko was planning to divorce him.[35]

John and May returned to Los Angeles once again, this time taking up residence at the Beverly Wilshire. Klaus Voorman, Keith Moon, and Harry Nilsson also stayed at the same hotel, and the four men frequently hung out together. One night they went to the Smothers Brothers opening. John, who had too much to drink, created a scene. The next day, a picture of John kissing May Pang headlined newspapers across the country, infuriating Yoko.

John was still not successful in his efforts to contact Phil Spector, and since he held the tapes, the album remained unfinished. John turned his attention to a solo album Ringo was developing. He wrote songs for Ringo and he began to work on songs for his next album, the first in six years that did not include Yoko.[36] The song "Whatever Gets You through the Night" was written around this time, as was a love song for May Pang called "Surprise Surprise" and "No. 9 Dream." Soon he began to pull these songs and a few others together into the album *Walls and Bridges*. *Walls and Bridges*'s single "Whatever Gets You through the Night," with Elton John on keyboards, went to number one. The song "Steel & Glass" was a put down to Allen Klein. The song "No. 9 Dream" was an attempt to reconcile with George Harrison. The dreamlike atmosphere of the song makes it one of John's best. Julian was visiting John while he recorded the album, and John sometimes took Julian to the studio with him. Julian played the snare drum in the recording of the song "Ya Ya." The credit on the album read: "Starring Julian Lennon on drums and Dad on piano and vocals." The album featured John's childhood artwork on the album cover and booklet, including a painting of boys playing soccer that was completed in 1952 when John was 11 years old.

Eventually John returned to New York City without May, hoping to reunite with Yoko, but Yoko refused him. Pang then joined John in New York, and they rented a penthouse apartment on Sutton Place, 434 East 52nd Street, with a wonderful view of the East River. John began to eat better and become healthier. They shared a regular routine together that began with coffee and newspapers in the morning and concluded when they retired to bed after *The Tonight Show with Johnny Carson*, one of John's favorites. John and May enjoyed walking around the city, window shopping, eating at favorite restaurants and binging on Whoppers, another of John's favorites.[37] Sometimes they would go to the movies to see popular films like *The Way We Were*. Emotionally, John seemed to be better as well. He resumed his relationship with Julian and began to correspond regularly with Aunt Mimi once again. He also socialized with Paul McCartney and with Mick Jagger, who was living on Long Island.

Once he was settled into his new place with Pang, John began work-ing on the *Walls and Bridges* album. Shortly after these sessions were underway, Al Coury, president of Capitol Records, paid Phil Spector for the tapes from the sessions John recorded in Los Angeles. John did not want to break stride with his new project, so he put the tapes aside for the time being.

When *Walls and Bridges* was coming out, Levy accused John of re-neging on his deal to produce an album of oldies to resolve the lawsuit. Levy was furious, but John explained what happened and assured Levy that the oldies album was in the works. John called together a group of musicians, and Levy offered his farm in upstate New York as a studio space. John gave him a rough copy of the album as evidence that the work was in progress, and Levy decided to publish it through his own record label, bypassing EMI and Capitol Records. Both EMI and Apple refused to agree to this arrangement, but Levy forged on and released the album under the title *Roots: John Lennon Sings the Great Rock and Roll Hits*. Levy then went on to sue Capitol, EMI, and John for breach of contract for $42 million.

It took two trials to resolve the lawsuit over this album. In 1975 the case was tried but a mistrial was declared. Levy sued John for not honoring their earlier settlement, and John sued Levy for issuing infe-rior products without John's permission.[38] John testified in court about the differences between a rough-cut track and a final mix. The judge awarded Levy $6, 795 in damages, and he awarded John $144,700.[39] The album was withdrawn from record stores. Shortly after this, John's finished version, *Rock 'n Roll*, was released. The album included songs like "Be Bop aq Lula," "Stand by Me," and "Ain't That a Shame," songs John enjoyed as a teenager in Liverpool.

TURNING BACK TO YOKO

On November 14, 1974, the stage production of *Sgt. Pepper's Lonely Hearts Club Band on the Road* opened. John attended with May. Yoko, who was just back from a tour of Japan, was also there, but John and May successfully avoided her. After the show, Yoko called May to tell her that she was thinking of taking John back.[40] May spent the night crying because she knew it was the beginning of the end of her relationship with John.

When John appeared at Madison Square Garden with Elton John on Thanksgiving, May's prediction came true. John gave an electrifying performance with Elton as the two sang "Whatever Gets You through the Night," "Lucy in the Sky with Diamonds," and "I Saw Her Standing There," which some interpreted as a gesture toward reconciliation with Paul McCartney.[41] But Yoko was in the audience. She sent John a flower backstage before the show and then met him afterward, joining John and May as they went out to a club after the performance. It was his final stage appearance.

John's time away from Yoko was one of the most productive music recording periods of his life.[42] John recorded more music during this period than he did in the 18 months prior to his separation from Yoko and the 18 months after his separation combined; however, John later characterized his time away from Yoko as barren and full of depression.[43]

By Christmas the Beatles' partnership finally dissolved terms. On December 19, the Beatles were all set to sign the agreement, but John refused. He finally signed on the 29th, and the dissolution became official on December 31.

NOTES

1. Elizabeth Partridge, *John Lennon: All I Want Is the Truth* (New York: Viking Press, 2005), p. 163.

2. Philip Norman, *John Lennon: The Life* (New York: Harper Collins Publishers, 2008), p. 683.

3. Albert Goldman, *The Lives of John Lennon* (New York: William Morrow and Company, 1988), p. 418.

4. Ibid.

5. Norman, p. 687.

6. Goldman, p. 436.

7. The Youth International Party, a radical counterculture group founded in 1968. Its followers were called Yippies.

8. Norman, p. 689.

9. Ibid., p. 691.

10. Ibid., p. 692.

11. Ibid., p. 694.

12. Ibid., p. 697.

13. Ibid., pp. 697–98.

14. Ibid., p. 700.

15. John Robertson, *The Art and Music of John Lennon* (New York: Carol Publishing Group, 1991), p. 157.

16. Goldman, p. 448.

17. Ibid., p. 451.

18. Norman, p. 707.

19. Ibid.

20. Robertson, p. 161.

21. May Pang and Henry Edwards, *Loving John* (New York: Warner Bros, 1983), p. 57.

22. Ibid., p. 6.

23. Norman, p. 714.

24. Ibid, p. 279.

25. Ibid., p. 720.

26. Robertson, p. 164; Norman, p. 721.

27. Pang and Edwards, p. 153.

28. Partridge, p. 177.

29. Pang and Edwards, p. 157.

30. Pang and Edwards.

31. Norman, p. 720.

32. Goldman, p. 475.

33. Norman, p. 724.

34. Pang and Edwards, p. 173.

35. Ibid., p. 174.

36. Robertson, p. 167.

37. Goldman, p. 663.

38. Norman, p. 745.

39. Ibid., p. 746.

40. Pang and Edwards, p. 267.

41. Goldman, p. 538.

42. Robertson, p. xii.

43. Ibid.

Chapter 9

GETTING INTO ANOTHER CAR

I'll outlive the bastards, in more ways than one.

—*John Lennon*[1]

Yoko called John just after the New Year to tell him she had quit smoking. John was impressed and wanted to do the same. He typically smoked two packs of Galouises cigarettes each day, something that left him short of breath and with a chronic cough.[2] Yoko called John to the Dakota on a Friday night to receive a special treatment she promised would help him to quit smoking. May begged John not to go. She had an uneasy feeling about Yoko's plans, but John went anyway. After John left, May tried to reach him at the Dakota, but Yoko intercepted her calls. Several days passed, and May did not see or hear from John. Then a few days later John showed up at his dentist's office for an appointment. May was in the waiting room because their appointments were scheduled months earlier for the same time, and she was shocked by his appearance. John's eyes were red-rimmed and he appeared to be quite disoriented, even zombielike.[3] When they returned to May's apartment after the appointment, John told her, "Yoko has allowed me to come home."[4] He packed a few of his things and left.

Once he settled back into the Dakota, John showed Yoko the diary
he kept when he was in Los Angeles, and then he burned it to symbolize
the new start he was making with her. Not all his friends were pleased
to see this reunion. When Mick Jagger heard the news that John had
returned to Yoko, he responded by saying, "I guess I've lost a friend."[5]
But it was official. John and Yoko made their first public appearance
a few weeks later at the Grammy Awards ceremony, where John presented the award for best album with Paul Simon. Olivia Newton-John
won, and Art Garfunkel accepted on her behalf, which led John to joke
with the former music duo about whether they were going to get back
together.

Early in the spring, Yoko announced that she was pregnant. John put
work on his record on hold in order to take care of her, although this
may not have been a huge sacrifice on his part since he was experiencing difficulty writing in the aftermath of his reunion with Yoko.[6] On
their anniversary, the two renewed their vows in their apartment at the
Dakota, dressed in white as they had been on their wedding day. It was
a Druid wedding ceremony to honor John's Celtic past. Yet in spite of
this public and personal commitment to Yoko, John continued his affair with May Pang off and on for the next three years.[7]

John's reunion with Yoko began the most reclusive period of his life.
He avoided public celebrity appearances, a pattern that continued for
the next five years, even though he was often seen in public as a private citizen enjoying a cappuccino or strolling through Central Park.
John was noticeably missing from public view on May 11, 1975, when
crowds gathered in Central Park to celebrate the last troops leaving
Vietnam. Other famous musicians and celebrities were quite visible,
including Paul Simon and Joan Baez, and given John's earlier efforts
to celebrate peace, it is difficult to imagine why he would avoid this
celebration, particularly when it was so close to his home.

But other more personal celebrations were soon to come. On John's
35th birthday, October 9, 1975, Yoko gave birth to his new son. John
and Yoko named the baby Sean Taro Ono Lennon. Sean is the Irish version of the name John, and Taro is a name given to the son who is first
born in a Japanese family. Elton John was named the baby's godfather.

The birth was not necessarily an easy one. Sean was born one month
prematurely by cesarean section. Albert Goldman claims that this was

done purposely because Yoko believed that if the baby was born on his father's birthday, he would inherit his father's soul once his father was deceased.[8] Sean had some health problems and was placed in intensive care when he was born. Because the baby experienced tremors, Yoko was tested for drugs just after Sean's birth, and the tests came back positive, but some report that this was because of the drugs she was given during the cesarean.[9] Others speculated that the baby suffered from drug withdrawal, but Yoko never made a public statement to confirm or deny this accusation. Four years later, she gave a donation to Hale House for Children, which treats babies born to mothers who are drug addicts.[10]

Once it was clear the baby and Yoko would be fine, John called Aunt Mimi to tell her about his newborn son and to share other happy news: the Immigration and Naturalization Service (INS) had at last stopped all proceedings against John, ruling that his 1968 cannabis conviction in the United Kingdom was an unfair basis for deportation. Further, the government could no longer deport John because he was the father of a U.S. citizen.

DISENGAGING

John's recording contract with EMI officially ended in 1976. Although he was offered several lucrative recording contracts with major record companies, he turned them down. It was the first time since 1961 that he was not under contract. Around this same time, Yoko began to take full responsibility for their business affairs. They decided to disengage from their creative work as Yoko focused on increasing their financial wealth. Her goal was to reach at least $25 million as Paul McCartney reportedly had done.[11] John decided to fully disengage from the music industry, canceling his subscription to *Billboard* magazine and avoiding all news about the music business.[12] Instead, he reportedly turned his attention to young Sean, focusing on his care and upbringing. He had help from Masako, a Japanese woman who became Sean's nanny. Masako and Yoko frequently conversed in Japanese, and John sometimes felt redundant as these two women took over the house and focused on Sean.[13] In spite of this, John did find ways to enjoy time alone with Sean. He took him in a stroller through Central Park, and he made it part of their routine to put Sean in bed at night. John sat by his son's bed and sang lullabies to the boy until he nodded off.[14]

While he seemed to be enjoying his private domestic life, John experienced a series of personal losses in 1976 that were quite troubling to him. First Mal Evans, the Beatles' long-time assistant, died in Los Angeles after being shot by Los Angeles Police Department officers in his girlfriend's apartment. This came as quite a shock to John, and after Mal's death, he went on a 40-day fast, consuming only fruit juice.

Soon after John's fast ended, he learned that his father was dying from stomach cancer. Alf seemed to have found happiness in the later years of his life, enjoying his marriage to Pauline and his role as father to David and the couple's second son, Robin. Much like John was doing with Sean, Alf had stayed at home to look after his boys while Pauline worked. John had a brief conversation with Alf on the telephone after he was admitted to the hospital, and he sent a bouquet of flowers with a card encouraging him to get well, but Alf died a few days later. After his death, Pauline sent John a copy of Alf's autobiography along with a letter Alf had written specifically to John. Alf included special notes to John throughout the book, hoping it would end the ill feelings his son bore toward him. Just a month later, Paul's father died, and soon after, Mater, John's favorite aunt, passed away.

In the midst of dealing with all these personal losses, John spent a considerable amount of time with his ongoing legal problems, including a lawsuit with Allen Klein. When the lawsuit was finally resolved, Klein was ordered to relinquish all managerial rights in exchange for a one-time payment of $5 million. John, with agreement from George and Ringo, invited the ever-loyal Neil Aspinall to the Dakota and asked him to oversee business at Apple. Aspinall's first reaction was to throw up in the guest bathroom, but he soon agreed provided he also had Paul's support. John guaranteed this, and Neil took the helm at Apple, leading the company to success that far exceeded anyone's imagination at the time.

John continued pursuing creative outlets in spite of his quite private life. He helped Ringo to finish recording the song "Cookin" for his album *Rotogravure*. Then, without a recording contract hanging over his head, he turned his attention once again to writing poetry and word plays, and to art, creating drawings and intricate collage work. John wrote a series of short pieces during this time that would later be compiled in a book called *Skywriting by Word of Mouth*. The book was in the same spirit and style as his first book, *In His Own Write*.

At the end of July, John was officially granted permanent U.S. resident's status, and he finally held a green card (which was a bit amusing to him because the card was actually blue in color). Now he could travel outside the United States without fear that he could never return. Yoko sent him on a trip around the world, but Liverpool was not on the itinerary.

THE RECLUSIVE WORLD TRAVELER

Many myths surround John's life in the late 1970s, some of which he and Yoko may have tried to perpetuate. He was often described as reclusive during this time, and he even described himself as a house husband who stayed home to bake bread, but John continued to come and go from his Dakota apartment at will. He and Yoko attended Jimmy Carter's inaugural ball, and they traveled extensively. When in New York, he could be regularly seen having a cappuccino or breakfast at La Fortuna, his favorite restaurant. John enjoyed regular visits from friends, even on occasion Paul and Linda McCartney, and his apartment at the Dakota was always bustling with people, some of whom were employees.[15] John took Polaroid photos of visitors to the Dakota, expecting that he would one day write a book and reminisce about all the people who had visited him.[16]

John had plenty of sources of entertainment in his apartment, and he sometimes chose to remain in his room for days at a time. He continued to be an avid reader and he enjoyed watching a large Sony television and videotapes of movies and comedy shows, including *Monty Python's Flying Circus* and *Fawlty Towers*.[17] He had extensive sound equipment in the apartment, although much of it was unpacked or waiting for a studio engineer to assemble for him.[18] He kept a cassette tape recorder close by to capture songs and fragments of ideas he might use in future work.

In 1977, Yoko, John, and Sean took their first family vacation to Japan, spending five months visiting Yoko's family and other sites in her home country. They were proud to introduce their new son to Yoko's relatives. Prior to the trip, John enrolled in a six-week Japanese course in Manhattan so that he could better understand the language. The Lennon family stayed at the Hotel Okura, and they spent time eating in restaurants, shopping, riding bikes, and visiting historical and religious sites. Although Yoko enjoyed having her family together, she missed Kyoko, whom she hadn't seen in four years, and she seemed to harbor some anger that she had never regained her social standing in her home country.

The trip to Japan cost John $700,000, and when he returned home to New York, he had to deal with his financial troubles. John owed the IRS money, so he sold his Flower Power Rolls Royce to get a $225,000 tax credit. John and Yoko also bought farmland to help avoid further tax problems. In a $2.7-million-dollar agreement, they bought three defunct and one working farm, equipment, cows, and bulls.[19] John seemed to like the idea of the farms. They reminded him of Scotland and the summers he had spent there in his youth. John planned to take Sean to Scotland in 1981 because according to numerology and astrology it would be a good year for their travel.[20] However, the farms did not resolve their financial problems, and in the end they only brought more tax problems and complications.

During the fall, John began to work on songs that would later be included in his *Double Fantasy (with Yoko Ono)* and *Milk and Honey (with Yoko Ono)* albums. Although he claimed when the *Double Fantasy* album was released in 1980 that the songs were inspired at the time, his home recordings indicate otherwise.[21] The songs on these albums were begun in the late 1970s and painstakingly rewritten and revised in the years before their release.

John seemed to be making a concerted effort to improve himself as a father, and he was certainly trying to be a better father to Sean than he had been to Julian. Although he was never very close to Julian and the geographic distance between them presented difficulties, he had not forgotten about him. John did see him on occasion, and Julian traveled from England to spend Christmas with John at the Dakota, even though he was never close to Yoko. There was snow in Central Park, and the two went sled riding together.[22]

MOVING ABOUT THE CITY AND ACROSS THE WORLD

There were some frightening and disturbing events John faced in the late 1970s. Someone attempted to blackmail John six weeks after he returned from Japan to New York City. The blackmailer threatened to kidnap Sean and demanded $100,000. John called the police and the FBI, and he insisted that Sean have an armed bodyguard wherever he went. Then in May 1978, an arsonist set fire to a barn, garage, and tool shed just as the Lennons were about to take control of a new property. More fires followed.

In spite of these events, John did not seem to be afraid. He moved freely and comfortably around the city that was now his home. He took Sean to the YMCA on West 64th Street regularly, teaching him how to swim.[23] He continued to push Sean in a buggy around Central Park, and he was often seen strolling there with Yoko. As he went about these mundane routines, people would sometimes recognize him and ask if he was John Lennon. His reply was typically "I get told that a lot," or "I wish I had his money."[24]

John also traveled easily around the United States and the world. He enjoyed time with Julian in Palm Beach, Florida, where he taught the boy to play the guitar. He flew Yoko and Sean to the Grand Cayman for vacation, and then a month later to Japan for their second family vacation there. Here John swam in the pool every day, and enjoyed shiatsu massages. He also spent time shopping for electronics and clothes.

Life at the Dakota changed quite a bit when the Lennons returned from their second vacation in Japan. Masako, who had joined the family on the trip to help care for Sean, decided that she should stay in Japan with her mother. This brought about a difficult period for Sean as John and Yoko tried to find other nannies. John described Sean as beautiful, and he loved and spoiled the boy. Sean was accustomed to having his own way, and it sometimes made it difficult for others to care for him. John did not want to send Sean to school, but he enrolled him in a nursery school when he was three; however, Sean was removed from the school as soon as he complained about it.

In September 1978, Yoko sent John to Hawaii. John ran into his old friend Jesse Ed Davis, and he fell into old habits, drinking a lot and doing drugs. When he returned from Hawaii, Yoko held a lavish celebration for John and Sean's birthdays at Tavern on the Green restaurant, just five blocks from the Dakota. After this, John retreated to his room again and resumed his use of heroin.[25] John spent most of the next 15 months in his bedroom.[26] Yoko claimed they were working on a musical, but John seemed to be writing songs that would later be used on the *Double Fantasy* album.

John did not receive money from Apple at year's end, and he faced ongoing financial problems. Yoko worried that John would be angry about the finances, but he did not seem to notice. He once said:

> Lots of people are addicted to money. People used to ask us this when we were the Beatles. We're not saying we never wanted to earn money, but the object was to be the best rock 'n' roll band, or be like Elvis, and the money was secondary. When we got it, it was just like what we'd read from other rich people saying, "Money isn't everything." They were right. It didn't do a bloody thing for you except get you on a plane instead of a boat. How many suits can you wear, or how much food can you eat?[27]

John gave Yoko power of attorney, which meant she would have complete control over his fortune and finances if he were to die.

John never was able to quit smoking, and by the late 1970s he was painfully thin, weighing only 130 pounds. When he was with Yoko, he adhered closely to a macrobiotic diet, believing this would help to offset the poor health effects smoking brought, but he also fasted and was physically inactive, spending most of his time in bed.[28] Although John had health ailments, he did not see a doctor. John Green, Yoko's tarot card reader and staff member, tried to convince Yoko to take John to a doctor, but she was worried he would be institutionalized.

EMPIRE BUILDING

As Yoko took increasing control over John's finances, she became obsessed with real estate. She added five units to their apartment in the Dakota, including Studio One, which consisted of two ground floor rooms, one of which became the office for Lenono Music, while the other served as a private space where Yoko worked each day. Yoko purchased another home called Iron Gate in the Catskills and another at Cannon Hill on the north shore of Long Island, where John spent a good amount of time. Cannon Hill had a swimming pool with an antique cannon beside it, as well as a private beach and dock. Fred Seaman, John's personal assistant, often traveled here with John and Sean because Yoko was busy with her work. Seaman soon realized that it was Yoko who had power in the relationship—Yoko made the decisions.[29]

But John did not seem to be concerned about money or the power relationships in his family. Instead, as he spent more time on Long Island, he turned his attention to sailing. John always loved water and enjoyed swimming, and from the time he was a child, the sea held a fascination for him. He began to read everything he could find about sailing and the ocean, and he hired Tyler Coneys from a nearby family-run marina to teach him to sail. Tyler stopped by regularly in the evenings when he was finished with work, and the two took John's boat into the bay. Sailing seemed to bring John much enjoyment.

In December Yoko purchased the El Solano, a 22-room mansion in Palm Beach, Florida that had once belonged to the Vanderbilt family. Julian visited John here on his 16th birthday. John chartered a small yacht for a birthday celebration, but news leaked to the public and a group of young women circling the yacht in a speedboat forced them to end the event early.

Yoko rarely made a personal or professional decision without consulting Japanese numerologist Takashi Yoshikawa.[30] She also consistently read tarot cards and consulted psychics, including John Green, aka Charlie Swan, who became a member of her permanent staff. John Green introduced Yoko and John to Manhattan art dealer Sam Green, who suggested the Lennons collect ancient Egyptian artifacts. They created an Egyptian room at the Dakota, and soon a gold sarcophagus, a carved receptacle for a corpse, became the centerpiece. Inside the sarcophagus reportedly was an Egyptian princess, a mysterious woman who had traveled from the East to marry a powerful Egyptian man. John and Yoko traveled with Sam Green to Cairo to view items from a newly excavated site, but after arriving in Egypt, they learned the dig was nonexistent. While they were in Cairo, John visited every museum and archeological site he could, and Sam Green later recalled that John believed he had lived there in a previous life.[31]

While John's absence from the public appearances created some intrigue about him, Yoko knew they could not remain completely out of the public eye. In May 1979, the couple ran a full-page advertisement in the London *Sunday Times*. They conveyed a message to the public that they were well and so was Sean, and that their silence was really an indication of love and not indifference. A few months later, the Lennon family returned to Japan for their third annual holiday. Afterward they made a pact to give up heroin.[32]

ROUGH SEAS AND NEW INSPIRATION

In February, the Lennons returned to El Solano to celebrate Yoko's 47th birthday. Yoko was still doing heroin, but John seemed to be either unaware of or unconcerned about this.[33] Yoko sent John and Sean to Cold Spring Harbor while she tried once again to kick the habit cold turkey. Sam Green tried to help Yoko to detoxify, and he encouraged her to return to art. Yoko tried to focus her attention on writing lyrics to songs, some of which would later appear in *Double Fantasy* and *Milk and Honey*.

John continued with his travels, and after a visit to Cape Town, he set his sights on a high sea adventure. John decided to sail for Bermuda. He left Newport, Rhode Island on June 4, 1980, aboard a 43-foot sloop called the *Megan Jaye*. Accompanying him were his young but experienced sailing teacher, Tyler Coneys, and his cousins Kevin and Ellen Coneys. The skipper was Captain Hank Halsted. He was close to John's age and had experienced the psychedelic rock world as a concert promoter, so John particularly enjoyed their conversations. John answered Hank's questions honestly, and when Hank asked John what he was going to do next, John simply replied, "I'm going to raise my boy Sean."[34]

At first the sailing was quite smooth and beautiful, with calm seas and dolphins swimming just off the bow of the boat. John was in charge of the ship's galley, and he regularly shared a watch with Tyler. But a few days into the journey a terrible storm blew up, complete with 65-mph winds and 20-foot waves. The Coneyses became seasick, and John had to help Hank navigate the boat, an act that established his status as a bona fide member of the crew. When Hank turned the helm over to his inexperienced shipmate, John rose to the challenge. He later told his personal assistant Fred Seaman:

Once I accepted the reality of the situation, something greater than me took over and all of a sudden I lost my fear. I actually began to enjoy the experience, and I began to sing and shout old sea shanties in the face of the storm, feeling total exhilaration. I had the time of my life.[35]

The seafarers successfully weathered the storm and passed through the infamous Bermuda Triangle before arriving at the island. Once John arrived in Bermuda, Sean, his nanny, and Fred Seaman arrived. John swam with Sean and enjoyed the sites and sounds of the beach.

The time aboard the yacht seemed to revive John's health and his creative powers.[36] He became tanned and appeared to me more fit, and he wrote two songs during the cruise, and then planned to write more. John claimed that he did not touch a guitar from the mid- to late 1970s, but tapes from this time prove otherwise. He played his guitar throughout this period, and in 1980, particularly after his time in Bermuda, he began to earnestly focus his attention on songwriting and creating albums.

John began recording his new album at the Hit Factory Studios on West 48th Street as soon as he returned to New York from Bermuda. He was fraught with insecurity as he ventured back into this world that was so familiar yet new to him, but it was quickly clear to the musicians that John was in charge. Rick Neilson of Cheap Trick traded guitar licks with John until they had just the right sound, and the group, which also included Cheap Trick drummer Bun E. Carlos, bassist Tony Levin, and keyboardist George Smalls, soon nailed the tracks in just a few live takes. While in the studio, John sometimes reminisced with the other musicians about the Beatles, but he tried to keep his thoughts focused on what was important to him and on getting the music just right. John taped a photo of Sean over the mixing desk as he worked on songs that were typically autobiographical and focused on love: "(Just Like) Starting Over," "Watching the Wheels," "Beautiful Boy," and "I'm Losing You." As the recording sessions came to an end each day, John made a point of returning to the Dakota to tuck Sean into bed before he went to sleep.

Yoko and John hired Jack Douglas to produce *Double Fantasy*. Jack had formerly worked with John and Yoko on the *Imagine* album when they recorded in New York, and after that he went on to successfully produce albums for Aerosmith and Cheap Trick. Yoko was clear from the outset that the album would include several of her songs, and she wanted the album to be her ticket to "honor and esteem."[37] John did not object; instead, he focused on making sure the album would showcase her talents as well as his own. *Double Fantasy* mixed seven of John's songs with seven of Yoko's. David Geffen released the album with his new company because he agreed to Yoko's proposal of a 50-50 split with John, even though this arrangement seemed to make John angry. The album's release was a huge public relations event, and many billed it as John's comeback. The single "(Just Like) Starting Over," John's first new release in five years, climbed the charts to number one in both the United Kingdom and the United States. To celebrate, John sent Aunt Mimi a pearl necklace and matching brooch.[38] With the album's release, John had renewed confidence.

Rather than take a break after *Double Fantasy* was finished, John contacted Douglas about getting back in the studio. He seemed to be reenergized and bursting with creative plans. He wanted to work on an album with Ringo, and he also wanted to establish his own recording studio on Riverside Drive, where he planned to re-record his standards. John was back in touch with George Martin and discussing plans to re-record several Beatles tunes, including "Strawberry Fields Forever." He continued to write new music, even composing the song "Street of Dreams" while stuck in traffic on 57th Street. Several of his last songs seemed to be preoccupied with death, including "Gone from This Place" and "You Saved My Soul."[39] John spent much of his time during the last two weeks of his life working on Yoko's single "Walking on Thin Ice" and shooting the video of *Double Fantasy* with Yoko in Central Park and in the studio.

The release of John's comeback album brought a flurry of attention from the media. *Playboy* interviewed him, and *Rolling Stone* writer Jonathan Cott and photographer Annie Leibovitz visited the Dakota in early December to capture John's story and image. Leibovitz photographed John and Yoko—her fully clothed with him naked clinging to her in a fetal position. On December 6, John gave BBC Radio 1 DJ Andy Peebles an interview, and then Leibovitz returned to complete her photo session in the afternoon on December 8. By all accounts, this was a happy, productive, and hopeful time in John's life, and this came across in his interviews as he discussed his house husband days and his plans for the future. John expected to soon return to England to visit Aunt Mimi, and he intended to bring the *Double Fantasy* musicians together in mid-December for rehearsals before taking them on the road for some concerts. Sadly, none of these dreams would be realized.

ETERNAL LIFE

On Pearl Harbor Day, Mark David Chapman waited outside the Dakota, like other fans who occasionally stood outside the ominous building hoping to catch a glimpse of John Lennon. Chapman remained until 10:30 AM, but when John did not appear, he left to get some lunch. On Monday, Chapman returned to his post at the Dakota and struck up a conversation with photographer Dave Goresh, who introduced Chapman to Helen Seaman and Sean. At the time, John was inside preparing for the photo shoot with Annie Leibovitz. He had been out earlier that morning, getting his hair styled into the Teddy Boy haircut of his youth after his usual breakfast at La Fortuna.

At 1 PM, John gave a radio interview to Dave Sholin, a San Francisco DJ at RKO Radio, and at 5 PM, he left the Dakota, autographing a copy of *Double Fantasy* for Chapman on his way out the door. Then, after working on Yoko's single for several hours, John and Yoko decided to go to the Stage Deli for dinner. As usual, however, they decided to first return to the Dakota so that John could say goodnight to Sean.

At 10:50 PM, the limo pulled up to the Dakota, and John stepped out onto the sidewalk. As he strolled toward the entrance of the building, Mark David Chapman called out "Mr. Lennon." Chapman assumed a two-handed combat stance and with a .38 handgun discharged five hollow point bullets. Four hit John Lennon. He stumbled into the Dakota, entered the porter's vestibule, and then collapsed on the floor. The cassette tapes he had been carrying scattered everywhere. Yoko followed him, screaming that John was shot. The porter rang the alarm for the police, and then covered John with his jacket.[40] He realized there was little he could do. The police arrived within minutes. They found Chapman standing outside the building calmly reading *The Catcher in the Rye*. His gun and the autographed copy of *Double Fantasy* were nearby. He did not try to run away or escape, although he probably could have easily done so.

One of the squad cars took John to the emergency room at Roosevelt Hospital on West 59th Street. Yoko followed in a second car. When John arrived at the hospital, he was no longer breathing and had lost over 80 percent of his blood. Doctors tried to save him, but it was soon clear there was nothing they could do. The hollow point bullets expanded upon entering his body, destroying organs and tissue upon impact, and there was no way he could have survived. John Lennon was pronounced dead at 11:07 PM. As the doctor's relayed the grim news to Yoko, she seemed incapable of processing the information, asking again and again if John was asleep.

Word of John's death quickly spread across New York and around the world. Within an hour of John's death, the street outside the Dakota was turned into a makeshift shrine as fans gathered, crying and looking around in disbelief. Some began to sing John's anthem "Give Peace a Chance" as they held candles and signs to express their sorrow. ABC sports announcer Howard Cosell interrupted coverage of a Monday night football game between the Miami Dolphins and the New England Patriots to disclose the tragedy to the American public. CBS

John Lennon is seen here in December 1980. This image was taken just a few days before his assassination. (AP Photo.)

anchorman Walter Cronkite interrupted regular programming to tell viewers that Lennon had been shot, and shortly afterward he confirmed that Lennon had died.

When she returned to the Dakota, Yoko called Mimi and Paul to tell them what had happened. Because of the time difference, it was December 9 in England, and Linda McCartney had just taken the children to school. She returned to find Paul sitting at the piano, shaking violently.[41] Paul phoned his former bandmates, and Ringo Starr, who was on vacation in the Bahamas with his fiancée Barbara Bach, called Cynthia, who was spending the evening with his ex-wife Maureen in London. Cynthia was shocked and devastated, and she left London immediately to return home to Julian, hoping to reach him before the media and others intruded on his privacy. Julian was just 17 years of age, the same age John had been when he tragically lost his mother, and this point was not lost on Cynthia. Cynthia and Julian spoke on the phone with Yoko, who arranged for Julian to leave immediately for New York. Soon after, Julian boarded an airplane where he was surrounded by newspapers that reported his father's death in headlines on the front page. When he arrived at the Dakota, Julian helped Yoko to break the news to Sean, and he tried to comfort his brother in the midst of terrible grief.

The news media sought out former Beatles for statements about their friend and former leader's death. Paul spent the day after John's death at the studio, and when he left, the press questioned him. Paul replied, "It's a drag,"[42] something he later he regretted. He explained that when he heard about John dying, he was stunned and didn't know what to say. He was also terrified, concerned about his own safety and the safety of his family. Paul later explained:

> I've hidden myself in my work, but [John's murder] keeps flashing into my mind. I feel shattered, angry, and very sad. It's just ridiculous. [John] was pretty rude about me sometimes, but I secretly admired him for it, and I always managed to stay in touch with him. There was no question that we weren't friends—I really loved the guy. John often looked a loony to many people. He had enemies, but he was fantastic . . . He made a lot of sense.[43]

Paul also remarked:

I talked to Yoko the day after he was killed and the first thing she said was, "John was really fond of you." The last telephone conversation I had with him we were still the best of mates. He was always a very warm guy, John. His bluff was all on the surface. He used to take his glasses down, those granny glasses, and say, "It's only me." They were like a wall, you know? A shield. Those are the moments I treasure.[44]

John's body was cremated at Ferncliff Cemetery in Westchester. There was no funeral, and it is not clear what became of the ashes. Some believe that Yoko has kept them, while others speculate that she sprinkled them in Central Park where the Strawberry Fields memorial she created in John's honor now stands.

Fans gathered in mourning in Central Park, Dallas's Lee Park, San Francisco's Marina Green, the Boston Garden, and countless other places around the world. Yoko asked them to come together the Sunday after John's death for a silent tribute to him. They complied. Thirty thousand gathered in Liverpool, more than 225,000 gathered in Central Park, and millions of others joined from various public and private places to observe 10 minutes of silence in John's honor. Yoko told the fans that John "loved and prayed for the human race . . . Please remember that he had deep faith and concern for life and, though he has now joined the greater force, he is still with us here."[45] After 10 minutes of silence, the song "Imagine" played over the speakers, and then the crowds quietly dispersed.

In the aftermath of John's death, Yoko had to ask fans not to give way to despair. She learned that two had already committed suicide, and she did not want more lives to be lost. She released a letter to fans explaining how she told Sean about his father's murder, and how she took him to the spot where John lay after he was shot. The young boy struggled to understand, asking why someone who liked his father would actually kill him. Sean cried and told his mother, "No Daddy is part of god. I guess when you die you become much more bigger because you're part of everything."[46] Yoko then turned inward, retreating to her bedroom where she mourned in private.

Rumors abound in the wake of a tragic death, and it is quite often difficult to sort truth from fiction in such cases. Some reported that Yoko was planning to divorce John in the months before his death.[47] Sam Habitoy, an interior decorator who was working on Yoko's apartment at the Dakota, moved in with her approximately six months after Lennon died,[48] and some suggest that Yoko considered marrying him. John's uncle Norman claimed that John was thinking of divorcing Yoko in his later years.[49] But it is difficult to understand what had always been a very complicated relationship between two very complicated people. John's personal assistant Fred Seaman later reflected:

> [John] was very tortured. He was somebody who was so divided, he really didn't know who he was. He didn't know what he wanted, and the way he dealt with it was by abdicating responsibility for his life and turning it over to Yoko, lock, stock, and barrel. He paid a very heavy price, as he said in the song "Woman": "My life is in your hands." He really believed that Yoko would take care of him, and he trusted her completely. He had blind faith, and I think he paid a very heavy price for that.[50]

John Lennon's cold-blooded murder seemed inconceivable to fans around the world. Chapman's official statement to the police began with the claim, "I never wanted to hurt anybody, my friends will tell you that."[51] The New York City Police Department took Mark David Chapman's word that he acted alone, and wrapped up their case. Chapman was sentenced to 20 years to life and locked away in the Attica State Prison John had so famously sung about years earlier.

Others were less certain Chapman acted alone. Writers Phil Strongman and Alan Parker suggest that Chapman, who was unemployed for much of his adult life, could not have acted alone. They point out that John and Yoko were again becoming involved with political activism, which included offering support for Japanese American workers who were striking for pay equity in San Francisco. They also note that John was eligible to become a U.S. citizen in 1981, something that would have allowed him to run for an elected office. They question the extent to which then-president Ronald Reagan and his administration may have viewed Lennon as a threat, not because John could have run for office as president, but instead because his beliefs were contrary to those held by the conservative administration. John was not afraid to speak out, even in the 1970s when he was living with the constant threat of deportation. What might he have done had he lived to enjoy the security that status as an American citizen might have offered? As Strongman and Parker analyzed similarities across the John Lennon, John F. Kennedy, Robert Kennedy, and Martin Luther King, Jr. murders, they raised important questions about why the British and U.S. governments still blocked the release of FBI files on Lennon 23 years after his death.

Family members, friends, and fans of all ages continue to mourn the loss of John Lennon and to find inspiration in his life and work, even though it is nearly 30 years since his death. Jello Biafra of the punk group the Dead Kennedys asked those who loved John to "Imagine . . . If John had lived,"[52] and unfortunately that is what we are left to do. We are left to imagine, to enjoy his music and art, and to take his and Yoko's words seriously when they asked fans to "Lift your eyes and look up in the sky. There's our message . . . We are all part of the sky, more so than of the ground. Remember we love you."[53]

NOTES

1. Phil Strongman and Alan Parker, *John Lennon and the FBI Files* (London, England: Sanctuary Publishing, 2003), p. 10.

2. May Pang and Henry Edwards, *Loving John* (New York: Warner Bros, 1983), p. 285.

3. Ibid., p. 291.

4. Ibid.

5. Ibid., p. 294.

6. Albert Goldman, *The Lives of John Lennon* (New York: William Morrow and Company, 1988).

7. Pang and Edwards, p. 309.

8. Goldman, p. 562.

9. Elizabeth Partridge, *John Lennon: All I Want Is the Truth* (New York: Viking Press, 2005), p. 185.

10. Goldman, p. 563.

11. Philip Norman, *John Lennon: The Life* (New York: Harper Collins Publishers, 2008), p. 750.

12. Norman, p. 751.

13. Goldman, p. 564.

14. Norman, p. 752.

15. Ibid., p. 764.

16. Ibid., p. 771

17. Ibid., p. 765.

18. Ibid., p. 766.

19. Goldman, p. 603.

20. Norman, p. 778.

21. John Robertson, *The Art and Music of John Lennon* (New York: Carol Publishing Group, 1991), p. 181.

22. Norman, p. 769.

23. Ibid., p. 767.

24. Ibid., p. 768.

25. Goldman, p. 610.

26. Robertson, p. 185.

27. Geoffrey Giuliano and Brenda Giuliano, *The Lost Lennon Interviews* (Holbrook, MA: Adams Media Corporation, 1996), p. 55.

28. Goldman, p. 605.

29. Giuliano and Giuliano, p. 212.

30. Norman, p. 773.

31. Ibid., p. 776.

32. Goldman, p. 624.

33. Norman, p. 788.

34. See Chris Hunt, Just Like Starting Over: The Recording of Double Fantasy, December 2005, http://www.chrishunt.biz/features26.html (accessed April 18, 2010).

35. Ibid.

36. Goldman, p. 643.

37. Ibid., p. 656.

38. Norman, p. 801.

39. Yoko later combined the songs that John recorded during the *Double Fantasy (with Yoko Ono)* sessions and these last days in the studio with her own work into an album released after John's death titled *Milk and Honey (with Yoko Ono)*.

40. Norman, p. 806.

41. Christopher Sandford, *McCartney* (New York: Carroll and Graf Publishers, 2006), p. 280.

42. Giuliano and Giuliano, p. 239.

43. Sandford, p. 9.

44. Bill Harry, *The Paul McCartney Encyclopedia* (London, England: Virgin Books, 2003), p. 505.

45. Partridge, p. 197.

46. Strongman and Parker, p. 177.

47. Giuliano and Giuliano, p. 21.

48. Ibid.

49. Giuliano and Giuliano, p. 194.

50. Ibid., p. 212.

51. Strongman and Parker, p. 150.

52. As quoted in Yoko Ono, *Memories of John Lennon* (New York: Harper Collins, 2005), p. 23.

53. Ibid., p. 176.

Appendix 1

CHALLENGES OF WRITING ABOUT JOHN LENNON AND EXPLANATION OF KEY SOURCES

The real Lennon was not the public statements he made.

> —*Harold Seider, as quoted in Albert Goldman,*
> The Lives of John Lennon, *1988*

Constructing a biography presents challenges for writers no matter who the subject or audience is. John Lennon is no exception. Readers expect truths, and there are certainly factual aspects of a life story to tell. In other words, identifying when John Lennon was born, where he lived, where he went to school, and other mundane details of his life is not too difficult. But capturing John Lennon's life in the particular times and places where he lived is more challenging, particularly for a writer who did not meet John Lennon and whose own life did not overlap very much with his. Paul McCartney once complained to Beatles biographer Hunter Davies about Philip Norman's biography of the band, pinpointing some of the challenges:

> In an earthquake you get many different versions of what happened by all the people that saw it. And they're all true . . . but how can you get the full story from someone who *wasn't* there, nor has talked to the main people?[1]

Hunter Davies, who spent countless hours with the Beatles in the height of Beatlemania, explained the challenges of capturing the life story of living people:

> Doing a biography of living people has the difficulty that it is all still happening. It is very dangerous to pin down facts and opinions because they are shifting all the time. They probably won't believe half the things they said in the last four chapters by the time you've read them.[2]

Davies noted some of the specific problems he faced sorting out the facts of John's childhood, and John later claimed that Davies's book was "bullsh**."[3] John's Aunt Mimi, who had primary responsibility for raising John when he was a young boy, told very different stories of John's early days than John told, and this was one reason John was dissatisfied with the book. For Davies, it was difficult to corroborate either version since Mimi's husband, George, and John's mother, Julia, had both passed away, and John's father, Alf, was absent from his son's life. Years later, John's half-sister Julia Baird penned a biography about John with writer Geoffrey Giuliano, and in some instances she relayed stories that were perhaps part of the family lore but that were later refuted. For example, Julia claimed that John was born during a German air raid on Liverpool, but reviews of historical documents and newspapers later revealed that there were no air raids on the night he was born.

More difficult than dealing with the facts and contexts is the interpretation of the story. Who was John Lennon the person, and who makes claims to understand him? How did John's private person intersect or not with his public persona? Many who knew John well noted that the public John was very different than the John they knew in private. People bring perspectives to their reading and writing of biographies, and some have specific agendas. Memories are problematic. Human stories are told from differing perspectives and with different alliances. For example, some biographers are more accepting of John's relationship with his second wife, Yoko Ono, while others clearly hold her in disdain. This influences their telling of John's story and the impact Yoko had on his life, creativity, music, and career.

John's story can be disturbing at times, but there are lessons to be learned from his complicated life, and there is no need to focus only his creative work and extensive accomplishments. Biography should provoke us and cause us to examine our own lives and priorities. We are all human, even the most famous among us, and so we are all riddled with contradictions, conflicts, and problems. John was troubled from the time he was a young boy, and his only father figure was his Uncle George. He was primarily raised by women who were a bit unusual for their time, and they doted on him. None of this excuses or explains away his misbehavior—John was smart and creative, and he worked to challenge himself and to change across the course of his life. This was perhaps most evident as he adopted Yoko's views on feminism and invested effort in being a better father to his second son, Sean, than he was to his first son, Julian.

There are many accounts of John's life and many sources that contribute to telling his story, from the interviews he gave and his own writings to the numerous biographies, films, videos of concerts, and tributes of John. None tell his story completely, and neither does this book. Instead, readers are encouraged to consider multiple sources and to read with careful attention to the credibility of each source. While a complete list of sources can be found in the bibliography of this book, some of the following may be of particular interest to anyone who wishes to obtain a more critical perspective about John Lennon and his music:

Hunter Davies's biography of the Beatles is a classic and should be read by anyone who seeks to understand anything about the members of this band. Davies spent countless hours with the Beatles and their families, and he interviewed friends and family members. Davies made some purposeful decisions about what to include and exclude from the book, taking some advice from John, who asked for edits after he read the first draft so that his Aunt Mimi would not be upset. Davies decided to omit any speculation about a sexual relationship between John Lennon and Brian Epstein because he personally did not believe it was true, and he did not want to hurt Cynthia or other members of John's family.

Albert Goldman provided a comprehensive biography that drew on six years of research, including more than 1,200 interviews with people who knew and loved John. Goldman was not enamored with Yoko, and she was not pleased with his book when it was published. Goldman wrote extensively about John's sex life, drug use, addictions, and violence over the years, but perhaps even more upsetting to Yoko were his criticisms of her. Some readers seem to question whether Goldman had the story or the facts right, and so this text, as any other, should be considered carefully against other books about John Lennon.

Two biographies to read against Goldman's are those by Ray Coleman and a recent work by Philip Norman. Coleman's biography is considered to be comprehensive, yet it perhaps errs on the side of idolizing John, certainly more than Goldman's text does. Norman was biographer for the Beatles and had a working relationship with Yoko Ono. His biography, while very detailed and comprehensive, takes a softer hand with Yoko. Norman's account of John's drug use, particularly in New York City, does not corroborate well with Goldman's.

Autobiographies and biographies of those close to John are also invaluable as they provide different perspectives on his life, particularly those by Cynthia Lennon and Julia Baird, as well as those written about Paul McCartney and George Harrison. Absent from this list is similar work by Yoko Ono. In her tribute to John Lennon, published in 2005, Yoko noted that she was not yet ready to write about her life with John, and she was not sure she ever would be. Instead, she continues to produce exhibits of his work and commemorations of his life.

John Robertson's work in *The Art and Music of John Lennon* contributes interesting information about Lennon's music in the context of his creative work with the Beatles and should be read by anyone who has a strong interest in the music John wrote.

Jon Wiener's book, along with a text by Phil Strongman and Alan Parker, chronicle John's complicated history with the FBI, raising provocative questions about the U.S. government's interests in John.

Elizabeth Partridge compiled an engaging photographic biography. She acknowledged the hundreds of sources that deal in some way with John Lennon's life, including books that print misinformation and what she refers to as "a few of the most deluded, trashiest books I've ever read, full of wild assumptions and sensational claims presented as facts."[4] She proceeds to note that one of the best sources on John

Lennon is John Lennon himself, particularly interviews he gave with trusted reporters. While I think she makes a good point, I also think John's interviews should be approached with an understanding of the contexts in which they were given. John Lennon had a quick wit and wry, sarcastic sense of humor. During interviews with reporters, he often joked around, adopting different voices, accents, and personas; therefore, the interviews he gave should not always be taken at face value. Writer John Robertson claimed that the John and Yoko interviews given in 1980 were intended to construct a story for the general public, in part to sell an album. He proposed that these interviews must be treated as creative works of art rather than expressions of honesty.[5] I agree—interviews John gave must be weighed carefully against multiple texts and contexts, but they are certainly worth viewing on YouTube and in print.

The Internet makes a host of original information available to viewers, and I certainly encourage those who are interested in learning more about John Lennon to view original clips of John's performances with the Beatles and later with Yoko, the Plastic Ono Band, and Elton John online. These performances are in many cases riveting and bring John to life in ways that text cannot. Further, John's writing and artwork can be found online and in various exhibits, and these sources also give a glimpse into his life, creativity, humor, and hopes. In his short 40-year life, he made an incredible impact on the world through his artistic and creative endeavors and his political activism, and it is certainly worthwhile to spend time attempting to better understand this complex and brilliant man.

NOTES

1. Hunter Davies, *The Beatles* (New York: McGraw Hill Publishing, 1985), p. 369.

2. Ibid., p. 339.

3. Jann Wenner, *Lennon Remembers* (San Francisco, CA: Straight Arrow Books, 2000), p. 84.

4. Elizabeth Partridge, *John Lennon: All I Want Is the Truth* (New York: Viking Press, 2005), p. 208.

5. John Robertson, *The Art and Music of John Lennon* (New York: Carol Publishing Group, 1991), p. xii.

Appendix 2

JOHN LENNON'S ALBUMS

WITH THE BEATLES

Studio Albums

Please Please Me (March 1963)
With the Beatles (November 1963)
A Hard Day's Night (June 1964)
Beatles for Sale (December 1964)
Help! (August 1965)
Rubber Soul (December 1965)
Revolver (August 1966)
Sgt. Pepper's Lonely Hearts Club Band (June 1967)
The Beatles (November 1968)—aka, the *White Album*
Yellow Submarine (January 1969)
Abbey Road (September 1969)
Let It Be (May 1970)

U.S. Albums

Introducing . . . the Beatles (January 1964)
Meet the Beatles! (January 1964)

The Beatles' Second Album (April 1964)
Something New (July 1964)
The Beatles' Story (November 1964), consists of documentaries and
    interviews
Beatles '65 (December 1964)
The Early Beatles (March 1965)
Beatles VI (June 1965)
Yesterday and Today (June 1966)
Magical Mystery Tour (November 1967)
Hey Jude (February 1970)

Canadian Albums

Beatlemania! With the Beatles (November 1963)
Twist and Shout (February 1964)
The Beatles' Long Tall Sally (May 1964)

Live Albums

The Beatles at the Hollywood Bowl (May, 1977)
Live at the BBC (November,1994)

ON HIS OWN

Studio Albums

John Lennon/Plastic Ono Band (December 1970)
Imagine (September 1971)
Some Time in New York City (with Yoko Ono) (September 1972)
Mind Games (November 1973)
Walls and Bridges (October 1974)
Roots: John Lennon Sings the Great Rock and Roll Hits (January 1975)
Rock 'n Roll (February 1975)
Double Fantasy (with Yoko Ono) (November 1980)
Milk and Honey (with Yoko Ono) (January 1984)

Experimental Albums

Unfinished Music No. 1: Two Virgins (with Yoko Ono) (November
    1968)

Unfinished Music No. 2: Life with the Lions (with Yoko Ono) (May 1969)

Wedding Album (with Yoko Ono) (November 1969)

Live Albums

Live Peace in Toronto 1969 (December 1969)

Live in New York City (February 1986)

Compilation Albums

Shaved Fish (1975)

The John Lennon Collection (1982)

Menlove Ave. (1986)

Imagine: John Lennon (1988)

Lennon (1990)

Lennon Legend: The Very Best of John Lennon (1997)

John Lennon Anthology (1998)

Wonsaponatime (1998)

Instant Karma: All-Time Greatest Hits (2001)

Acoustic (2004)

Peace, Love and Truth (2005)

Working Class Hero: The Definitive Lennon (2005)

The U.S. vs. John Lennon (2006)

Remember (2006)

SELECTED BIBLIOGRAPHY

PRINT RESOURCES

Baird, Julia, and Giuliano, Geoffrey. *John Lennon, My Brother.* New York: Henry Holt and Company, 1988.

Coleman, Ray. *Lennon: The Definitive Biography.* New York: Harper, 1992.

Davies, Hunter. *The Beatles.* New York: McGraw Hill Publishing, 1985.

Emerick, Geoff. *Here There and Everywhere: My Life Recording with the Beatles.* New York: Gotham Books, 2006.

Fawcett, Anthony. *John Lennon: One Day at a Time: A Personal Biography of the Seventies.* New York: Grove Press, 1976.

Fontenot, Robert. "Did John Lennon Have Any Signs of His Impending Death?," http://oldies.about.com/od/oldieshistory/f/lennondeath.htm (accessed December 14, 2009).

Giuliano, Geoffrey. *Blackbird: The Life and Times of Paul McCartney.* New York: DeCapo Press, 1997.

Giuliano, Geoffrey, and Giuliano, Brenda. *The Lost Lennon Interviews.* Holbrook, MA: Adams Media Corporation, 1996.

Goldman, Albert. *The Lives of John Lennon.* New York: William Morrow and Company, 1988.

Harry, Bill. *The Paul McCartney Encyclopedia.* London, England: Virgin Books, 2003.

Julien, Olivier. *Sgt. Pepper and the Beatles: It Was Forty Years Ago Today.* Hampshire, England: Ashgate Publishing, 2008.

Lennon, Cynthia. *John.* New York: Crown Publishers, 2005.

Lennon, John. *In His Own Write.* New York: Penguin Books, 1964.

Lennon, John. *Skywriting by Word of Mouth.* New York: Harper: 1986.

Norman, Philip. *John Lennon: The Life.* New York: Harper Collins Publishers, 2008.

Ono, Yoko. *Memories of John Lennon.* New York: Harper Collins, 2005.

Pang, May, and Edwards, Henry. *Loving John.* New York: Warner Bros: 1983.

Partridge, Elizabeth. *John Lennon: All I Want Is the Truth.* New York: Viking Press, 2005.

Robertson, John. *The Art and Music of John Lennon.* New York: Carol Publishing Group, 1991.

Sandford, Christopher. *McCartney.* New York: Carroll and Graf Publishers, 2006.

Strongman, Phil, and Parker, Alan. *John Lennon and the FBI Files.* London, England: Sanctuary Publishing, 2003.

Thomson, Elizabeth, and Gutman, David *The Lennon Companion: Twenty-Five Years of Comment.* New York: Schirmer Books, 1987.

Wenner, Jann. *Lennon Remembers: The Rolling Stone Interviews.* San Francisco, CA: Straight Arrow Books, 2000.

Wiener, Jon. *Come Together: John Lennon in His Time.* New York: Random House, 1984.

Wiener, Jon. *Gimme Some Truth: John Lennon FBI Files.* Berkeley: University of California Press, 1999.

ELECTRONIC RESOURCES

John Lennon: Official Web site (http://www.johnlennon.com).

John Lennon FBI Files (http://www.lennonfbifiles.com/).

Rock and Roll Hall of Fame (http://www.rockhall.com/inductee/john-lennon).

Rolling Stone (http://www.rollingstone.com/artists/johnlennon).

INDEX

About the Author

JACQUELINE EDMONDSON is associate dean for undergraduate and graduate studies in the College of Education at Penn State University. She has written several biographies for Greenwood Press, including *Jerry Garcia* (2009), *Jesse Owens* (2007), *Condoleezza Rice* (2006), and *Venus and Serena Williams* (2005).